WILD HORIZONS

Overleaf: A forest fire in the Okavango Swamp created unusual light effects for filming.

WILD HORIZONS

Dieter Plage

COLLINS
St James's Place, London
1980

William Collins Sons & Co Ltd
London · Glasgow · Sydney · Auckland
Toronto · Johannesburg

First published 1980
© Sandy Shore Investments S.A., 1980

ISBN 0 00 216029 3

Set in VIP Bembo
by W. & G. Baird Ltd, Antrim
Designed by Marian Morris
Maps drawn by Brian and
Constance Dear
Made and Printed in The Netherlands
by Smeets Offset, Weert

To Mutti and Vati

Of the Cruelty of Men

Human creatures will forever be fighting
and killing one another. They will destroy
the vast forests of the world and when
they are filled with food they will deal out
death, labour, terror and banishment to
every living thing. Everything on earth or
under it or in the waters will be pursued,
disturbed or spoiled or removed from one
country to another.

Leonardo da Vinci

ACKNOWLEDGEMENTS

This book would not have been written without the encouragement of the late Sir William, and Lady Collins.

My thanks to: David Farrer, for his tireless help in correcting my grammatical mistakes, and for his criticism of, and suggestions for, the final draft; Peter Hartmann, who taught me the basics of filming; Prof. Dr Bernhard Grzimek, whose films have influenced my entire life; Aubrey Buxton, Chief Executive, Colin Willock and Mike Hay, Executive Directors of Survival Anglia Ltd, who gave me the chance to film in Africa and, therefore, to write this book; people like Willy Zeintl at the Arriflex factory in Munich, who through their ingenious inventions make our films possible.

No film would be complete without mention of the Survival staff at Park Lane. To use Colin Willock's words, they 'put together all the rubbish I shoot'.

A special thank you to Bernabe de La Bat and Consul Dr Karl Heinz Schneider.

Thanks also to: Mike Amos, Bob Aschmann, Jean Pierre von der Becke, John Blower, Melvin Bolton, Herbert Bourn, Terry Briceland, Derek Bryceson, John Burmeister, Alan Coulson, John Dixon, General Mebratu Fissaha, Bob and Jenny Grunsell, H. E. Sultan Ali Mirah Hanfare, Eldred Hapelt, Darryl Hecht, Pat Hepburn, Frank Hill-Mathews, Bill Holz, Ismail Mohamed Ismail, Tim Jefford, Dr Mary Jensen, Benjamin Kanza, Paramount Chief Lethsolathebe Moreme I, Jacques Midgeotte, Rolf Olles, Horst G. Oppel, Mick Pollock, Attila and Karen Port, Jack Ramsden, Stoffel Rocher, Carl and Gisela Schlattholt, Ras Mengesha Seyoum, Chander Sharma, Mike Slogrove, Helmut zur Strassen, Gahuranji Tanganika, Laurence Tennant, Dr Jacques Verschuuren, Raymond Werksmann.

And of course my special thanks to the characters who appear in this book.

Goetz Dieter Plage

CONTENTS

ILLUSTRATIONS

Unless otherwise stated, all photographs were taken by G. Dieter Plage (Bruce Coleman Ltd.).

MAPS

Prologue

In March 1945 a nine-year-old boy was playing with a band of companions on the banks of the river Elbe, where the spring floods had left ponds behind them. The children's games were rudely interrupted by the arrival of a ragged battalion of German troops fleeing eastwards from the advancing American tank columns. Before crossing the river the soldiers threw away all their arms and equipment, including some handgrenades which one of the older boys, already a member of the Hitler Jugend, knew how to prime. What fun to throw them into one of the ponds and see what would happen!

What did happen was a series of loud explosions, then mountains of water shot into the sky filled with the shining bodies of fish. The explosions subsided then and there, spread over the surface, were hundreds of fish, big and small, dying or dead.

The nine-year-old who had taken part in this holocaust experienced a sudden and violent revulsion against the wanton waste of animal life: a revulsion – centred on such activities as big game hunting – which has remained with him all his adult life. This nine-year-old was, thirty-four years later, me.

Before the war my father had been a First Wireless Officer, serving on many ships from cargo boats to luxury liners – he was in the *Bremen* when she won the Blue Riband for the fastest trans-Atlantic crossing. But his favourite run was the African one, and I loved to hear the stories about his experiences there. Once when sharks surrounded his ship at Lourenço Marques (now Maputo), he and some other members of the crew gaffed one of them; and in its violent struggles to escape it smashed the ship's rail. He told me about going on a safari. Best of all, he had a photograph album and an illustrated book about Africa. This was my constant delight. Pictures of wild animals, of all the wonders of tropical Africa, stories about bananas you could actually pick off trees. I believe that the seeds of my future were sown at a very early age.

After serving as wireless operator and pilot with the Luftwaffe, my father was captured and held in a prisoner-of-war camp in Schleswig-Holstein. By this time Germany had been divided and my mother and I were living on the other side of the border in the Russian occupied zone. The Russian troops were rough, tough and dirty. But in many ways they were also very childish. My grandfather had given me a brand-new, shiny bicycle bell which I had fixed on my decrepit old bicycle. One day I was riding through the town proudly ringing my bell when I passed a Russian soldier on a brand-new machine which had no bell. He stopped me, seized my old bicycle and pedalled off, merrily tinkling the bell, leaving me with his gleaming new bicycle.

On another occasion some Russians were bivouacked under a tree a hundred yards away from our house. At that time we got our water from a tap on an outside wall. The Russian soldiers ordered my grandfather to detach the tap and screw it into their tree. It took a high-ranking officer to explain to the soldiers that this would not work.

In the course of four years my mother crossed the heavily-policed frontier seventeen times, taking our few remaining possessions with her, so that we could join my father in the then British Zone and start a new life. On seven occasions I went with her. The first time we took the train that runs along the border between the East and West zones. It stopped frequently, but each station was guarded by East German police. At last we pulled in to a station where there was a high embankment opposite the platform. My mother and I threw our cases out on to the embankment and jumped down after them; but my mother was careful to close the door behind us. If she had not the police would have discovered our escape as they carried out their routine search of the train, and we could have been arrested. As it was the train moved on, we kept well hidden until the police dispersed, and then we scrambled to safety.

A year after the war ended our family was reunited and my father became an engineer with the West German Ionosphere Institute. We lived at first in an old castle near Preetz in Schleswig-Holstein, where the Institute had its temporary headquarters. The castle was owned by an old lady, the Baroness von Donner. Long ago she had owned a big estate in what is now Tanzania and was then German East Africa. She showed me black and white photographs of wild life, and a colour film of a giraffe walking through a sunset, which kept alive my fascination with Africa.

At the age of fourteen I saw the two great films made by Professor Dr Bernhard Grzimek and his son Michael, *No Place for Wild Animals* and *Serengeti Shall Not Die*. They so fired my imagination that I determined to become a cameraman devoted to the cause of conservation.

Somehow I acquired an Agfa box camera. What I longed for next was a film projector! But my father was sceptical. The idea of being a cameraman was probably just a temporary whim of a fourteen-year-old; he was determined that I should go to university. He refused to help. So my friend Heinz Reiter and I approached a number of photographic dealers – how could we make a projector? All of them scorned us until at last a man who owned a camera shop took pity and was very understanding. He actually told us how a projector could be made, and Heinz and I made one. It didn't work, of course, but my father was reluctantly convinced. He gave me a sixteen-millimetre hand-wound projector and my brother the necessary film to project; it was a Western called *The Attack on the Gold Express* and it ran for seven minutes.

My father's African photograph album was my constant delight.

The first night we tried out our new toy, we ran the film eight times. Finally our parents packed us off to bed, where we continued to run the film until we fell asleep.

My young brother Gunter then developed an unexpected business sense. He sent out notices to all the boys in our block of flats and to family friends, inviting them, on presentation of the notice and payment of one pfennig, to witness our film. The pfennigs did not exactly roll in, but my savings enabled me, with my father's considerable help, to buy an Eumig C 3 movie camera, the first to have a coupled light meter.

Soon after this I was appointed projectionist at my school. I hired films from the government educational film department, timing their showing whenever possible to coincide with my Latin lessons, which I loathed. I spent every minute of my spare time with Peter Hartmann, the photographer in the government film department, who taught me all the basics of film making. His patience was inexhaustible, and I owe him an enormous debt of gratitude.

I left school at the age of sixteen, and my father was so upset that he told me I would never make good. I took up an apprenticeship in photography at Photo-Hauschildt in Darmstadt. My teacher there was the camera dealer who had been so helpful when I wanted to build a projector – Will Hauschildt. He was hard and sometimes ruthless, sometimes kind, the perfect combination for a successful business man. He taught me many things with an incredible thoroughness. Largely thanks to him I came top in my exam.

But how was I to get to Africa? One of the first requirements for going to Africa was to become fluent in English; so I answered an advertisement for a photographic instructor to the American forces based at Babenhausen, near Frankfurt-am-Main. I held this unlikely post for nearly a year, and whilst working there I met the managing director of a large department store in Cape Town. He offered me a job as a salesman in its newly established photographic department, at a salary of £50 a month. I accepted. The firm advanced me the fare from Rotterdam to Cape Town, which I had to repay at £5 a month. So in 1958 I sailed for the 'promised land'.

My arrival in South Africa marked the beginning of eighteen years in that continent. At first, when I was working largely on my own, it was not easy. Often I had to eke out a tin of beans between my morning and evening meals. I could of course have asked my father for help, and he would have given it. But I was too proud, too determined to make good on my own.

After some time in Cape Town as a salesman I was sent to the store's East London branch, where I was made manager of the photographic department. During my stay I had several wonderful chances to photograph strange people and customs. The most remarkable of these I chanced upon was undoubtedly the rite of circumcision practised by the Xhosa tribe in the Transkei.

What I witnessed, and recorded on film, was the circumcision of four youths aged between sixteen and eighteen. When the local witch doctor arrived, the youths were led out to meet him. He sharpened his spear on a stone, then the foreskins of the youths were pulled out to the fullest extent. The witch doctor made his first incision, and cried 'Are you a man?' In each case the answer came, 'I am a man'. A second incision was followed by the same question and answer. Finally came the third incision, when the foreskin was totally severed. The same question, the same answers. The youths showed no sign of the suffering they were enduring, for stoicism was their passport to adult society. Cowards would be banished for ever from their community.

Their penises were bound up with herbs and ointments, and the youths were returned to their hut, where they would stay for four weeks. Traditionally they had, during this time, to hunt for their own food, but this custom has now been given up.

After four weeks they were brought out, their naked bodies covered with a glaze of white clay, their heads shaven. Their hut and all their possessions were immediately burned behind them. The youths proceeded to the river, where they washed themselves clean. When they emerged they were given new white blankets and sticks, and allowed to rejoin their family and tribe.

I am told that since I witnessed the ceremony it has been rendered more antiseptic; a real doctor, in addition to a witch doctor, is present, but the rite and principle survive.

My assignments at East London, however, proved for the most part humdrum, so I applied for a job as an assistant cameraman with a film producer whom I shall call Mr Big. Mr Big was a strange, violent character. I realized later that he tended to paranoia, and was visited often by delusions of grandeur. He was a film producer of near-genius, and he certainly introduced me to some wild horizons. He also gave me the benefit of working with his other assistant, Rodney Borland, who became a great friend and colleague of mine.

Mr Big usually made wild life films which showed capture operations or people 'frim framming' animals. He did not have the patience to sit for weeks in a hide and photograph the real wonders of nature. The type of film he made had been popular since the war, and remained so up to about 1967; but the public then began to demand more serious documentaries.

At the time there were too many elephants in Kruger Park and the Department of National Parks had decided to cull some of the family units. That was where Mr Big came in. The plan was to capture twenty baby elephants by darting them from a helicopter, and ship them to the United States. Rodney and I went with Mr. Big to film the operation.

The Kruger biologist, Dr Pienaar, flew low over the bush in a helicopter, ready to dart the elephants with his crossbow. One day as we were following the helicopter in our pick-up truck we saw it gain altitude abruptly, indicating that an elephant had just been hit. Seconds later the whole herd came rushing towards us through the bushes. They swerved to the left and screamed and trumpeted around our vehicle. But as they moved off a little elephant calf was left behind, running slowly and swaying from side to side. He lifted his trunk and screamed to attract the attention of his mother, who was about fifty yards in front. She stopped in her tracks, turned round and trumpeted. Another young cow also stopped. Both swung round and went back to the calf.

Just as the cows arrived the little body fell in a pathetic heap. The elephants tried to pick up the young fellow and put him back on his feet, but he simply collapsed again. Another trumpet made the rest of the herd stop and scream with rage, and they came back, charging our cars, and stopping only a few yards away. Then they moved up to the fallen baby and formed a defensive circle around him.

The situation now was really serious. The drug the biologists were using, M99, mixed with the tranquilizer Hyacine, causes the pupils of the darted animal to dilate. If the vet did not get to it in a very short time the animal's eyes would suffer permanent damage. We all advanced towards the elephants guarding the baby. This made the cows even more aggressive, and more determined in their efforts to get the baby back on its feet. The commotion had caused so much strain on the cows that they put their trunks up into their mouths and sucked liquid from their stomachs, spraying it behind their ears and on to the baby elephant, to keep cool.

The vet in charge of the ground operation called on the helicopter to drive away the adult elephants, in order to get at the baby. As the helicopter approached most of the animals fled in panic, but two cows remained. The machine hovered about ten yards from the brave little group. One cow departed but the mother stayed. The helicopter stood directly above her, enveloping her in a hurricane of dust. But still she stayed.

Then the helicopter began to descend, and the incredible happened: the mother reared up on her hind feet and lashed out at the machine, nearly grabbing its skids and pulling it out of the sky. Terrified, the pilot immediately ascended to a safer height. Again the brave cow faced her adversary. Looking up, she placed herself in front of the baby; and while she slashed about with her trunk she tried to lift the baby on to its feet with her hind legs.

An immediate decision was called for. After a brief exchange between the ground crew and Dr Pienaar it was decided to dart the cow as well. A feeling of deep sadness came over me, and I suggested that after the heroic fight the cow had put up we should let the baby go. The others agreed. But still the cow had to be darted. Again the helicopter swooped low, and Dr Pienaar shot the dart into her shoulder. Again she tried to attack the machine. Five anxious minutes passed, then slowly the cow became drowsy and went down next to the calf. Immediately the doctor moved in and gave both animals the antidote – M285. Moments later they started to get up, a bit drowsy at first, but quite unharmed. The mother nudged the baby with her trunk for reassurance and they both moved off into the bushes. I could not help the tears in my eyes: it was one of the most extraordinary scenes I had ever witnessed.

During the time I worked for Mr Big, he taught me an enormous amount. In particular, however difficult it might be, to use a tripod. There was no comparison, he said, between the effect of a picture taken from a fixed object and one taken by a cameraman on the move, or even stationary. The hands would tremble – particularly, for example, in the face of a charging rhino – and the result would be flickering and blurred. He used to say that if any of his cameramen had filmed the assassination of President Kennedy without using a tripod, he would have thrown the film in the waste bin. This made Rodney and me very aware of the necessity of using a tripod at all times. The quality of the result spoke for itself.

My first real opportunity to prove myself as a cameraman, however, proved disastrous for my relationship with Mr Big. It happened in Rhodesia, where there was also an elephant problem. Elephants carry tsetse fly, purveyor of sleeping sickness, although they themselves, like many other mammals, are immune to the disease. The south of Rhodesia was free of tsetse fly, and a fence had been erected running east and west across the country to stop the fly moving south. But elephants sometimes broke through the fence, carrying the dreaded fly with them. So periodically tsetse fly-infested elephants living close to the fence on the southern side were driven back through the fence into the north of the

Overleaf: As the helicopter descended towards the drug-darted baby elephant the mother bravely stood her ground.

country. The drives were conducted by the park ranger from a light aircraft per radio. It was my good luck, or so I thought, to be given the job by Mr Big of photographing one of these operations.

It was not easy. While Mr Big watched from a helicopter the elephant hunters drove at about 30 mph through thick bush that tore our clothes and obscured our view. In a comparatively open space I saw an angry elephant come charging straight at us. The driver swerved violently and the elephant passed by; but we collided with a tree at full speed. The camera equipment was ruined, my leg badly gashed, and my tripod almost stunned me as it collapsed. When I finally limped through the gap in the fence to the dry river-bed where Mr Big had landed I was in poor shape. Mr Big was furious. Had I taken *any* film? Yes, I replied, and then described what had happened, how the camera and the tripod were broken. Mr Big stormed at me, reviled me, swore at me. It was the last straw. I resigned on the spot.

After my break with Mr Big, an out-of-work cameraman with little cash to his name, I returned to Germany and wrote to Professor Grzimek asking him for a job. He advised me to go to his friend Aubrey Buxton (now Lord Buxton), executive director of Anglia Television. With a measure of reluctance Mr Buxton agreed to see me if I would bring samples of my work to London. I met him and left the films at his office – and spent an agonizing night and morning of suspense. When the phone finally rang I picked it up apprehensively. It was his secretary who told me my appointment was at noon. He greeted me with the words, 'How nice to see you! Your films are marvellous, just what we're looking for! Would you like a drink?'

That question marked the beginning of my real career. I was given a one-year contract at first and a generous advance for buying the expensive equipment I would need. The films I made for Anglia Television over the next eleven years are now shown in a hundred different countries all over the world; and making them took me to some of the strangest and most beautiful parts of the African continent.

This book is not an autobiography – it is not a chronological account of my film-making – it is simply about the places I visited, the friends I made, and the wildlife I photographed in eighteen years in Africa.

PART ONE *Botswana*

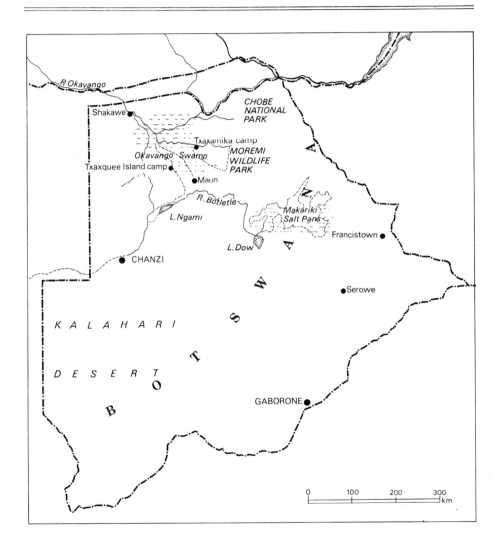

1 The Idyllic Swamp

The word 'swamp' has ugly connotations. It conjures up visions of endless mud, stinking vapours, a place that is useless – and dangerous. But most Europeans who have been there – and not many have – agree with me that the Okavango Swamp in Botswana is about as near to paradise on earth as you can get.

To me Okavango means lakes of glass-clear water, white sandy islands shaded by palms where wild game play undisturbed, and fish hurrying for cover under papyrus reeds as a dug-out glides slowly through channels cleared by hippopotami. This is my favourite region in all Africa and I returned here again and again during my eighteen African years.

The mighty Okavango river has many peculiarities, not least the fact that it never reaches the sea. It gathers in the catchment area of the Angolan Highlands, winds through dense jungles in southern Angola, crosses the Caprivi Strip in South West Africa and spends itself in the barren, sandy wastes of the Kalahari Desert in the Republic of Botswana. In doing so, it forms a swamp delta six thousand square miles in size.

Fed by the yearly rains in Angola, the river rises above its banks in the rainy season and its flood moves south. It reaches the village of Shakawe in May. From there the river forms a maze of islands, reedbeds and papyrus channels. It is a paradise for game and birds and a wilderness as yet untouched and unspoilt by man.

The dense papyrus beds filter the water, so that it reaches the middle of the swamps crystal clear. During the months of May and June the flood progresses slowly southwards, reaching Maun about the end of June. From then on the gigantic mass of water flows on through the Botletle River, the southern outlet of the swamps. The Botletle ends up in Lake Dow and the Makarikari Saltpans, where it evaporates.

Between Shakawa in the north and Maun in the south, a distance of over one hundred and fifty miles, the elevation varies only by a few feet. Therefore the flood moves very slowly, and spreads over a vast expanse of swampland.

On my first visit to Okavango, in 1965, I set off on a safari trip from Francistown with three companions – Eldred Hapelt (Happy) from Rhodesia, a German girl called Inge Toepperwien, and an African, Boyce – to drive to Maun, nearly four hundred miles away across the Kalahari Desert. We were hoping to make a film in the newly developed Moremi Wildlife Reserve.

The heat was almost unbearable. The only relief was one wayside store which sold iced Coca-Cola. Two dust-choked days out we glimpsed greenery on the horizon; and in a few hours we were suddenly enveloped by the lushness of trees as we crossed a small bridge and reached our destination.

Maun was at that time a small village, the only major buildings being the local Riley's Hotel with its inevitable pub, where big game hunters tell the tallest stories over a bourbon or a beer, the District Commissioner's office, the hospital and the house of the Paramount Chief of the local Batawana tribe.

At the pub I was introduced to the Paramount Chief himself, Lethsolathebe I, the President of the Ngamiland Fauna and Flora Conservation Society. Over a beer we discussed the possibility of making a film at Moremi. He assured me of his full co-operation and introduced me to the capable Warden, Jack Ramsden, whom I was to meet again in the years to come. Jack was very helpful, and after granting us permission for filming in the Reserve, he sent us on our way with the best of luck. The final leg of our journey was a sixty-five mile trip through deep sand to the gates of the Moremi Reserve.

On the way we encountered Africa's greatest game conservationist, the tsetse fly. Because it is the carrier of sleeping sickness it has been called the scourge of Africa. For humans it may be – its stinging bite can be very annoying – but for wild animals it has been a saviour in many parts of Africa, holding the advancing herds of cattle at bay. Without it the Okavango would be no paradise.

I was therefore horrified, on a later visit to Okavango, to come across large numbers of bright red drums marked 'Dieldrex' standing in the forest and on the banks of streams. The swamps were to be sprayed with this deadly insecticide in order to eradicate the tsetse fly. Without proper scientific control, this could be ecologically disastrous.

Apparently the tsetse fly had recently moved into an area just across the Thamalakane River from Maun. Surveys showed that the area occupied was about two miles by half a mile. Because it was so close to the town, and dangerous to the local cattle, it had been decided to eliminate the pocket of flies by spraying it with Dieldrex, and ring-barking all the trees in the area for a period of about seven days.

I managed to get hold of the official report on the project, which revealed alarming figures. After the spraying the dead bodies of wild animals had been collected by the ring-barking gangs. One hundred and nine birds of twenty-one different species were found, and twelve mammals. The search was abandoned ten days after spraying.

These figures are at first misleading. Under these conditions Dieldrex would remain deadly to wild animals for about two months. Larger mammals would have been scared out of the area, disturbed by the noise of the sprayers. Scavengers would have removed many carcases before they could be found. Many birds would have devoured poisoned tsetse fly that were still capable of flying, and then died their painful death elsewhere. Clearly, also, the denseness of the local vegetation would have concealed a large proportion of the dead bodies. Considering how small an area was sprayed, the figures are extremely high.

Rachel Carson warned as long ago as 1962, in her *Silent Spring,* of the dangers of large scale insecticides then being used in North America. Poisons like Dieldrex can have a catastrophic effect on local fauna; and little is known as yet about their possible side effects, such as sterilization and increased susceptibility to disease. But at the time of my first visit to Okavango it would have seemed inconceivable that man might wantonly threaten the life of this idyllic place.

At the gates of the Moremi Reserve we picked up our guide, a charming young Herrero called Notice. Apparently when his father came to the local registrar's office to record the name of his son he had not made up his mind what to call him. On the wall he saw the name '*Kiziso*', the local equivalent of the English word 'Notice'. And that is how Notice got his name.

At that time there were no roads in the Reserve, and Notice guided us through thickets of palm trees, plains with herds of red lechwe, buffaloes, impalas, zebras and of course elephants. The fiery sun was already going down as we reached the camping place that Notice had chosen, beside a clear stream.

While everyone else was eagerly unloading the car, I took a stroll among the little islands of gently swaying palm trees. I wanted to make sure we really had the best camping site. About a quarter of a mile away I could see another water channel, where some hippos were calling. A fish eagle flew up and settled on a tree, eyeing me cautiously. I raised my binoculars and saw, at the edge of another cluster of trees, a herd of buffaloes grazing. I was glad they were so far away. The call of a Pels Fishing Owl rang out from the crown of a large fig tree. A slight breeze swayed the palm trees. My eyes drank in the beauty all around me, and I soon forgot the rigours of the long journey.

As I went on the grass got thicker and higher, until it reached my waist. I had to cross it somehow in order to get to the main channel; I followed a game trail well trodden by antelopes and buffaloes. I was watching the spoor closely, and all at once I came across the clear track of a lioness in the dust. It was very fresh. But perhaps because I was tired and my back ached from the long journey I ignored it and went on. All I wanted was to get to the water and have a cooling bath.

Fifty yards further on the grass parted and the lioness leapt towards me. I froze. There was not time to think. Fifteen feet away from me she snarled and went into a crouch. The main thing was not to run. Run and you are dead. These thoughts raced through my mind. Keeping a close eye on me she slowly stretched out her front paws, somewhat nervously shuffling her hind feet into the right position to jump. Her ears folded back and her tail flicked from side to side.

I looked down into the yellow eyes looking up to me through the yellow-brown grass. I knew she was about to charge again. I tensed my muscles. Her purring growl became louder. We were eye to eye.

Then I took a gamble. Shouting as loud as I could, arms stretched out, 200 pounds of angry Plage charged the startled beast. She jumped up only six feet in front of me and leapt out of sight. At the same time the grass came alive with lions and another seven charged away into the nearby forest patch. The scent of a kill hit me and I realized that I had walked into a group of lions which hours before had killed a buffalo cow. I sat down, trembling, on a fallen tree and watched the lions disappear. All I could think was 'What a pity that I didn't have a camera!'

Later on, with no-one else about and the sounds of the bush around us, we talked contentedly long into the night. As I lay on my stretcher I watched the stars twinkle in the clear sky. A satellite moved slowly from west to east, symbolizing a different world. In the distance I heard the howl of a hyena and the growl of a lion. This was the true Africa, the Africa described by the old explorers. This is how they must have felt. I fell asleep.

Suddenly a hand was shaking me. It was Notice. 'Sir, Boyce has been bitten by a snake!' I tried to ignore him; it must be a bad dream. But again he shook me, his voice almost frantic. I realized then that it was reality.

To me Okavango means lakes of glass-clear water and white sandy islands where wild game live undisturbed.

I leapt from my stretcher. Happy was feeding the fire with new logs which threw glowing ash into the night sky. In the flickering light I saw Boyce lying under his blanket, his face swollen like a balloon. His eyes were mere slits. He could hardly breathe, and his forehead was bathed in perspiration. His normally happy, smiling face was contorted with pain and very pale. I told myself: just stay calm and try to do the right thing. I asked Notice whether he had seen the snake. He said no, it had happened while he was asleep. Probably it had been a night adder. By now Happy had brought the First Aid box, which contained the anti-venom. To my horror I found that the bite was just below Boyce's left eye. The first rule for snake bites is to tie off the bloodflow towards the heart with a tourniquet. But in this case it was impossible. What was I to do? A quick glance at the instruction pamphlet gave me a shock: 'Facial bites – consult physician at once. Almost always deadly!'

All sorts of horrific visions crossed my mind. Suppose I gave Boyce an injection and he died? I saw myself hanging for murder! There was a spooky silence about the place, interrupted only by the croaking of bullfrogs and a jackal's howl. Happy's hands were trembling as he held the torch. I tried to calm myself. I realized that I had to act if Boyce was

going to live. I broke the first ampoule and filled the syringe with ten cc of serum. With my left hand I gripped the skin around the bite and pushed the needle in. By now Boyce's body was shivering in spasms. I injected five cc around the bite, pulled out the needle and gave another five cc into the neck muscle. Then I injected another ten cc of serum intramuscularly into the arm, for at that stage I had no idea how to inject intravenously.

I realized that the next few hours would be vital and that I had done everything I could under the circumstances. We put Boyce into a comfortable position. All at once the stress was too much for me. A dark blanket seemed to cover my eyes and I almost passed out. I held my head low and the blood returned to my brain, then I sank exhausted on to my stretcher. I told Notice to wake me if complications developed – as if I would have known what to do – and immediately fell into a deep sleep.

I woke up as the sun was rising, still wondering if the ordeal of the previous night was a bad dream. To make sure I looked around and saw to my immense relief that Boyce was moving under his blanket, and the swelling had gone down considerably.

The hippos of Okavango conveniently clear channels through the swamps which are then navigable by canoe.

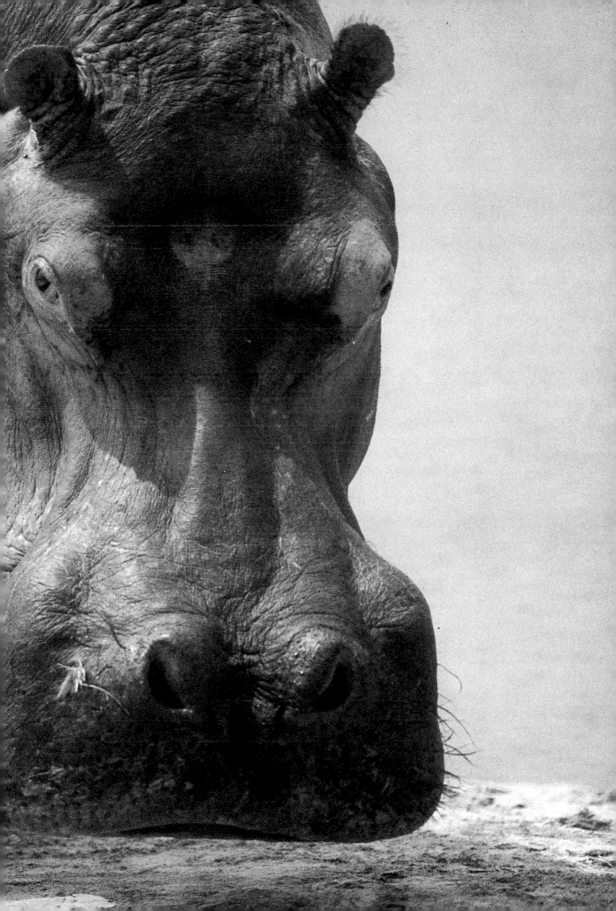

We all agreed that in any case we should get Boyce to the hospital in Maun. And we had a stroke of luck: in the distance we heard a car approaching. It was a safari guide returning to Maun with a client. We told him what had happened and he offered to take Boyce with him. We heard later that Boyce made rapid progress and within five days was allowed to leave hospital.

We spent the remainder of our visit to the Moremi in exciting foot safaris, observing and filming buffaloes and elephants. Although the animals were very shy, the sheer beauty of the forests and the clear waters had a magic all their own.

There is a saying in Maun that if you have once drunk Okavango water, you will always come back. My second visit was with Rodney Borland under the banner of Anglia Television.

Rodney and I had remained great friends since our Mr Big days, and when I started working for Anglia he agreed to become my assistant. Soon after we began working together Rodney married a beautiful girl called Moira. She was the same shape as Raquel Welch. Moira came with us to the Okavango and on one occasion she nearly sank a boat.

Rodney and I went one morning to a hide which we had set up on one of the numerous hippo channels that twisted their way through dense papyrus thickets. We had arranged that Moira would fetch us at lunch time. She set out from our base camp, standing upright in the boat, and raced through the channels and hippo trails with her magnificent hair blowing in the wind. All she had on was a very small bikini. Unbeknown to her, about half a mile away, a large boat was labouring upstream, filled with a dozen Rhodesian farmers, singing and brandishing beercans. Having sipped beer all day, they were quite intoxicated. They had come to this paradise to get away from it all. As they approached a tight bend in the river, Moira suddenly raced past them, looking like some young goddess. They were so perplexed that they crashed into the riverbank, cracking the bow of the boat.

Minutes later Moira reached our hide. We laughed when she told us what had happened. On the return journey we decided to hide her under the canvas front of the boat. As we approached the scene of the shipwreck, Rodney and I stopped. The farmers had managed to put some tape over the crack and were about to launch the boat again. They were laughing. When they saw us one of them said indistinctly, 'I told you, you're all drunk, it was a man after all. You're seeing things.'

From the moment Moira appeared on the scene, our lifestyle changed. She added a lady's touch. There were always flowers and a table cloth on the table. When there was no wind we even had candles; and so a meal was always a special occasion. We had a great time together, which I will always cherish.

Rodney, Moira and I had come to the Okavango this time to make a *Survival* film about crocodiles. We were based at Bobby Wilmot's crocodile camp near Maun. Bobby Wilmot and his team of hunters probably hold the world record for the number of crocodiles they have shot – forty thousand in twenty years. But since the Botswana Government restricted him to one thousand a year Bobby had abandoned shooting and started this tourist camp.

The white man who survives in the African bush, and actually flourishes, must be a good deal larger than life. He must be brave and self-reliant. He must be able to improvise, to suffer great hardships, to run great risks. He must be prepared to be a loner, may well be prone to outbursts of violent temper. He must be able to lead and win the allegiance – and often love – of the Africans who work for him. Such a man was Bobby Wilmot. He also became my very good friend.

From Bobby I soon discovered that in my absence from the Okavango a serpent had entered my Garden of Eden. It took the shape of a dredger. What harm could this dredger do? Ostensibly it was cutting a test channel that would increase the flow of water through the swamp. And yet . . .

Botswana had an excellent record in the field of conservation, as witness the Moremi Wildlife Reserve, which the authorities plan to join up to the much bigger Chobe National Park in the north-west of the country, making an almost complete ecological entity. But Botswana is, the Okavango apart, an almost waterless country, dominated by the Kalahari Desert. And now, only one hundred and fifty miles from Maun, a rich diamond field was being exploited – a mine which when fully operative would swallow millions of gallons of water daily. Where could this water come from? Only from the Okavango Swamp. And if this happened then my paradise would be drained of its life-blood – and another ghastly error made in the name of progress.

Wilmot's camp was sited at Txaxanika, on the shores of a big and very beautiful lagoon, inside the Moremi Reserve. Rodney and I began to reconnoitre. At first we dived with aqualungs and an underwater camera. We swam and swam, but though there were plenty of fish there was no sign of a crocodile. So we borrowed Wilmot's aluminium boat (a full-grown crocodile will bite right through a rubber dinghy) and went deeper into the swamp.

It is possible to catch a small crocodile round the neck, but we were after bigger stuff, and what we found was more than we had bargained for. It was a twelve-foot specimen. Now the two essentials for crocodile

catching are: first, dead silence while you approach him; and then, a spotlight. The reason for the first is obvious: you must drift up to the crocodile without alerting him to danger. With the spotlight you can pick out the two gleaming cat's eyes of his snout above the water line.

We took this giant by surprise, and Rodney was able to pass a loop under the crocodile's mouth. The result was impressive. As I steered the boat above him he rose as if on tiptoe out of the water, snapping wildly and viciously. The two Africans with us were terrified, but Rodney managed to throw a rope in the shape of a figure eight over the crocodile's jaws, forcing his mouth shut. Then our lamp went out. In the ensuing pandemonium the crocodile managed to break free from the noose and escape. Perhaps it was just as well.

Next day we had better luck. We managed, by the same methods, to catch a seven-foot crocodile and drag him captive up the bank. Then we built two strong underwater fences, enclosing nearly fifty yards of the channel. I got under the water and, when I was ready, Rodney released the crocodile into the stream. I drifted backwards with the current until my feet touched the downstream fence, my body kept buoyant by the current. The crocodile passed right under me. I followed, still filming, and saw the crocodile vanishing into a hole in the bank. Desperately I grabbed its tail. The crocodile emerged, bit savagely at the waterproof casing of my camera and made off.

We were still eager for more crocodiles. Next time we set out in a very strong rubber dinghy, powered by a twenty horse-power engine and manned this time only by Rodney and me. Suddenly we saw two large eyes in the dark; was it a really big croc? Slowly we moved forward. Rodney was about to switch off the engine when we realized that we were face to face with a bull hippopotamus. He was approaching us head-on in a channel which left no room for two-way traffic.

In an attempt to scare him we put on full throttle. He was unimpressed. For perhaps five seconds he stood half a yard out of the water, then dived and made straight for us.

Rodney accelerated and the light boat surged forward, heading for the place where the hippo had submerged. As the animal passed underneath us we heard a series of sickening bumps. We were now simply drifting, and the hippo turned in pursuit. Fortunately Rodney had a flash of inspiration. He lifted the screaming twenty horse-power engine out of the water and turned its exhaust gases straight on the charging beast. It was enough. The hippo turned tail and fled.

Two Okavango hunters: the crocodile and,
perched on a branch above him, the fish eagle.

I was sitting beside a camp fire in the Okavango in 1969 when I heard the radio transmission of a man's first landing on the moon. With me were Rodney and three Africans, including Notice, who could speak English. We were transfixed by the words coming out of the small speaker. I looked up. It was a full moon, bright and clear in the night sky. As I looked at it I heard Neil Armstrong say '. . . one small step for a man, one giant leap for mankind'. A new era had begun.

I looked at Notice, staring into the glowing embers. I said that the voice we had just heard was from two men who had landed up there, on the moon. Notice looked at the moon and said, 'No sir, it is impossible. It is far too small.'

Rodney and I had returned to this land I consider the most beautiful in all Africa to film the pied kingfisher. We had been asked by Anglia to submit material for inclusion in their projected film of the Duke of Edinburgh's visit to Africa.[1] It was to consist of stunning shots of the wild unlikely ever to be repeated. Now it is quite easy in the Okavango to take a photograph of a pied kingfisher, even of the bird diving to catch a fish. It was another matter to film the actual catch underwater, for it was impossible in a given stretch of water to guess where the bird would hit it and at what angle. There was the added difficulty of refraction by underwater light.

Rodney and I decided to narrow the odds by building a plexiglass tank inside the water and filling it with fish, so that the prey would at least be confined to one place. We put the tank under a favourite perch of one kingfisher. The camera in an under-water housing was placed under the tank. All we had to hope was that the bird would dive into our tank filled with fish. It took about three weeks but finally we managed it successfully. We got a magnificent sequence, and it was shown, together with other material selected by Anglia, in *Now or Never*.

One day Rodney and I set up a hide close to the bank of a swamp stream, from which to photograph the activities of two malachite kingfishers. They were making a tunnel into the opposite bank by repeatedly flying at it. Both of our cameras were pointed at the opening. Suddenly I heard a rustling noise close beside me. I moved my head very slowly to the left, and found myself staring at a black mamba about one foot away. I froze.

It is commonly held that a snake's eyesight is bad. It cannot focus clearly, but reacts instantly to movement. This snake was upright, its tongue flickering. We stared at each other for what seemed like an eternity, but was probably less than a minute. I was certain that it would

[1] *Now or Never*, 1971.

strike. I knew that if it did I would have two to three minutes in which to get the serum into me, otherwise I would not have a chance. All I could do was remain motionless. The mamba swayed to the left, then slid out of sight through the gap between the hide and the ground.

Bobby Wilmot was not so lucky. Back in South West Africa three months later I was told how he died. Apparently he jumped out of his boat on to the bank of one of the Okavango streams to reach his car, which was parked on one of the more or less dry stretches of the swamp. A black mamba lying on the bank struck him. Bobby had just one ampoule of serum in the boat. Shocked and already in pain he broke the ampoule and spilt the serum.

In agony he staggered to his car and drove for a while (neither of his African companions could drive). Then he got out of the car and told Elias, his cook, what was to be done with his belongings. He died within minutes. He was buried on the site of one of his crocodile camps. The Africans said that the spirits of the swamp had taken his life because he had killed too many crocodiles.

2 The Cry of the Fish Eagle

Of all the birds of prey in Africa my favourite is the fish eagle. Its haunting cry echoed in my ears long after I left Okavango, and I resolved that I would return one day to film this marvellous bird.

The Cry of the Fish Eagle (1975) was undoubtedly the most ambitious film I had yet attempted. Although I was determined to shoot the film in Okavango, I went first to study the bird at another of its habitats, Lake Naivasha in Kenya.

I was accompanied on this trip by Leslie Brown, the eminent ornithologist, who had agreed to help me make my film. Leslie is famous the world over: his *Eagles, Hawks and Falcons of the World* and other books are classics; and he has won further fame by his study of the flamingo colony on Kenya's Lake Natron. When Kenya was still a colony he had been its Chief Agricultural Officer. When I first met him he was a free-lance consultant for a number of international organizations, including the World Bank.

Leslie is a tall broad Scotsman, with an impressive beard and the reddish skin that is the badge of so many of his countrymen. He is totally fearless, and he accepts with glee any challenge to his inventiveness. He does not give a damn what he says to man, woman or beast. He is the perfect companion to have beside you in stormy times. As both mentor and friend I owe him enormous gratitude.

Lake Naivasha is perhaps the loveliest of all the Rift Valley lakes of East Africa. Leslie Brown lived not far away, on the outskirts of Nairobi, and some years previously he had started to make a survey of the lake with his fellow-conservator John Hopcraft. He astonished me when he said that they had identified no less than 284 pairs of fish eagles here,

Previous page: A camera mounted in a remote controlled aircraft gave us excellent close-ups of the fish eagle in flight.

making it certainly one of the largest, if not *the* largest colony in all Africa.

As our boat glided slowly through the papyrus islands of Naivasha, I was impressed by the wealth of wildlife the lake supported. There was the startling malachite kingfisher with its characteristic head-bobbing, exploding into colour as it streaked across the water like a miniature jet plane, homing in on its fish target; a goliath heron on its spindly legs, watching carefully; and then a pair of fish eagles, soaring and calling.

On our way back to the jetty we saw an osprey hovering above the water, then diving steeply, disappearing and then surfacing with a large fish in its claws. I was amazed that a fish eagle population of such density should tolerate an osprey in its midst. In the Okavango I had seen the fish eagles' hostility to other birds of prey. Perhaps the richness of the fish population here meant that there was enough for everyone. Another difference between the two locations was that while the fish eagles of Naivasha lived amicably together, however close their nests, in Okavango there was fierce territorial jealousy, even between parent birds and their own offspring.

Although Leslie had immediately agreed to help me make my film he could not at first understand why I wanted to make it in Okavango. Why, he said, go all the way there, when here, at hand, were far more fish eagles, far more easily got at? I was determined, however; Lake Naivasha was too civilized, surrounded by cultivation, irrigation and human interference. Leslie finally yielded to my arguments – no mean feat on my part considering the force of his character. But he was only convinced I was right, I think, when he reached Okavango and saw the unbelievable beauty of this wild region.

The fish eagle film marked a new advance in the fortunes of Anglia Television: the beginning of the US version of the *Survival* series. For years Anglia had been trying, with scant success, to break into the American market, by far the largest in the world. The company's chief executive, Aubrey Buxton, was a man of brilliant business acumen, and he refused to accept defeat. In 1971 he won the interest of J. Walter Thompson, the biggest advertising agency in the United States. They teamed up and founded the company known as Survival Anglia Inc., registered in New York.

I proposed the film to Colin Willock, the *Survival* writer, pointing out that the fish eagle was a close relative of the American bald eagle. It was also a bird of prey, always a popular subject. Colin gave me the go-ahead.

The fish eagle called for the sort of detailed organization I had never before attempted. Some people tend to think that to make a film of wildlife in the African bush all you have to do is to walk about with a

*The fish eagle takes the bait: he looks as if he is moving
slowly, but he is developing about as much energy
as a bullet from an elephant rifle.*

camera and a guide. In fact it is a highly technical and complicated
operation, often taking months or even years to prepare and complete,
requiring infinite patience and great gifts of organization. We were lucky
to be able to film the fish eagle in four to five months, not counting the
long period of preparation. The one thing a wild life cameraman should
never be asked to do is to give a fixed date for completing a film, as –
unlike cameramen filming people – he has no control over his subjects.

From the first I decided that the key to the whole film was to get shots
of the fish eagle actually on its nest. But how? The fish eagle nested in
trees between forty and seventy-five feet above the ground.

I suddenly remembered that my brother's passion in life was building
model aeroplanes, and that he and a friend of his had developed a method
of radio control from the ground that enabled an aeroplane to be powered and guided, with a camera, also radio operated, mounted on the
front. I asked Gunter and his friend Winfried Franzke if they would join
our expedition, and they enthusiastically agreed. Gunter insisted that the

model aircraft must be a float plane, proofed against forced landings on Okavango's innumerable channels and lakes. So far, so good. With this means of following and photographing the fish eagle in flight we hoped to achieve marvellous results.

What I wanted, however, to complete the picture, was a means of filming the fish eagle from above, of watching it not once but many times on its nest. In other words, a copy of a fish eagle's nest, higher than the real thing. Fritz Fey, a German engineer living in Windhoek, came up with the idea of building a collapsible tower. The material consisted of units of square tubing with aluminium braces which would make up snugly into a single item. We purchased the material in South West Africa. Fey also supplied us with light cables which would prevent the 'nest' from swaying with the winds. From Germany we brought two rubber boats equipped with fifty horse-power Mercury engines to help us move all our goods out into the swamps.

When we arrived in Okavango we visited Lloyd Wilmot, Bobby Wilmot's son, at the crocodile camp near Maun. He advised us to set up camp at a small island called Txaxquee, about a hundred miles north of Maun. The island was deep in the reeds and papyrus country criss-crossed by hippopotamus trails. These trails were the only way of approaching it, but it was easy to take a wrong turning.

Lloyd and I first inspected the site in one of the crocodile camp's boats, and though I had Lloyd with me it took three and a half hours. With our faster boats, when they arrived, we got there much quicker. The trick was to determine the right load, then let the boat's powerful engine lift the prow out of the water in order to plane over the surface.

These boats were a great boon; but there was one problem: mine would not start.

Although the engine had 'Thunderbolt' ignition, which was reputed to start 'at the first pull', I had terrible trouble with it and frequently had to resort to removing the spark plug and squeezing a little petrol into the combustion chamber via the plug hole. This was time-consuming – and a real nuisance in an emergency. After I had had the engine serviced several times I got pretty fed up and decided to write to the Mercury manufacturers as follows:

Dear Sirs,

I am the proud owner of a fifty horse-power Mercury engine, with Thunderbolt ignition. Unfortunately I have great difficulty starting it. I have had it serviced and checked many times but the same fault occurs. Lately, when I go into Riley's pub in Maun, people say 'here comes the

Mercury man', because my right shoulder has developed disproportion-ately larger than my left one, with the constant pulling on the engine.

I should be grateful if you would send me details and prices of a left-hand conversion kit so I can expand my left shoulder to match.

An early reply would be appreciated.

Yours sincerely, etc.

I *did* get a prompt reply, saying that the Mercury people found the letter very amusing and I should send the engine to their agents at Johannesburg for a complete overhaul 'on the house'.

Txaxquee was an amateur fisherman's paradise. The water around it was crystal clear, the peace and quiet absolute. It was shaded with great fig trees, under which on this visit was pitched our tent. The water abounded in fish; all you had to do was cast your spinner and you could reel in a fat bream.

Eventually the whole team and all our equipment were installed in the camp. Rodney, Winfried and Gunter assembled Gunter's remote-control aircraft, and the following morning we had a trial run. We set off in the two fast boats. In one were Rodney as pilot, Winfried holding the plane with the camera on it and Gunter in control of the transmitter; in the other Leslie and I, waiting to film the take-off. Both boats accelerated until there was enough lift to launch the plane. It flew at tree level, guided by the transmitter, and circled round a lagoon. Gunter pressed the button on the transmitter which activated the camera. In a nearby tree sat a fish eagle which we had been assiduously feeding, so that by now it was half tame. The plane got quite close to it before it flew away, and the camera gave us almost a close-up. Then the plane's engine cut out and it dived steeply into a tree. Fortunately Gunter was able to repair it so that we could continue filming.

This semi-tame fish eagle was, on his own account, an expert fisher-man. He was no longer afraid of us, and we were able to get shots of him at fairly close range. But to film him actually catching a fish was another matter. For one thing, it was impossible to predict with any degree of accuracy the angle at which he would swoop. So, as with the pied kingfisher, we prepared a perspex tank in which we placed a live bream. The fish eagle took the bait. While I waited with Leslie in a specially built hide the bird began his gentle downward glide.

On the shores of the lagoon we saw fish eagles
snatch fish out of the beaks of lesser birds.

In Leslie's own words, as the fish eagle dives on his prey, 'he looks as if he is moving slowly, but he is developing about as much energy as a bullet from an elephant rifle. If he were to strike an unmovable object with such force he would break his legs. As he takes the bream therefore he will throw his legs forward just before he strikes, till his talons open inches in front of his head, and as he passes over the fish, strike down and backwards, pulling it out of the water behind him without hurting himself.'[1]

One morning on our way to the hide Leslie and I saw a pair of fish eagles soaring in the clear blue sky. Circling each other in ever-widening arcs they suddenly flew together, locked their talons and cartwheeled towards the water, spinning round at increasing speed like an aeroplane going into a spin. About a hundred and fifty feet above the water they let go of one another, and just above the surface they pulled up and called.

This mating display of the fish eagle is one of the most exciting sights in the world of birds. Leslie Brown had already described it in ornithological circles and was at first met with scepticism. I considered myself lucky to have seen it, and was only disappointed not to have been able to film it, as it happened too suddenly.

As I watched the fish eagles flew together again and landed on a tree about forty-five feet from another pair. Both pairs started calling violently, throwing back their heads and giving out their wild, characteristic cry. Suddenly the two males flew up, passed each other twice, and locked talons, tumbling into the grass, while the females went on calling. It was clearly a territorial dispute. When the males settled again in the tree the females rose from their perch and chased each other round and round. Then one pair mated while the other couple called violently. The other female suddenly dived at a branch, broke it off with her talons and returned with it to build up last year's nest. Her mate followed her. It was the nest we had been filming for the last few days.

From where I was watching it took me five minutes to reach and climb the eighty feet to my own special hide high up in a tree. No sooner was I ensconced than I heard the female calling quite close. Right in front of me were a few old weaver nests. The female came in a fast dive right at my hide, banked at the last second and grabbed one of the weaver nests with her talons. She landed on her nest, ripped it apart with her talons and beak, and lined her new nest with it. When she had finished the male joined her. As they stood on the rim of the nest he caressed her, preening the feathers under her beak and down her throat. Madame then continued with the rebuilding of her nest, while Monsieur, probably feeling

[1] From Colin Willock's *The World of Survival*, André Deutsch, 1978.

that he was in the way, took off and landed on one of the perches near the water.

Silence followed. Then abruptly there was a new outburst of violent calling. Searching for the reason I saw an immature fish eagle about two years old in a tree about a hundred yards away. The mother eagle took off and dived steeply on her offspring. She snatched him out of the tree and the two of them went tumbling in wide somersaults towards the lake. When the mother momentarily loosened her grip her offspring managed to escape into a thorn bush. Thereupon the father dived and tried to pull the young bird out of the bush, while the female circled overhead.

Eventually the desperate youngster managed to struggle out of the bush, but while he was crossing a small patch of grass towards the next bush I heard a frightening hissing sound as his father, talons locked, came in a power dive to knock his child flying. In a last bid for safety the young fish eagle managed to fly into another thick bush fifty yards away. Mother and father circled above but seemed to be satisfied. It seems that when fish eagles start their second breeding they lose interest in their first family and chase the young ones out of their territory.

With the film taken from the hide and from the remote-controlled plane my task was now half accomplished; but I was still determined to make use of Fritz Fey's tower to survey and photograph another fish eagle's nest. Leslie and I selected a forty-foot-high nest which we had seen on our first reconaissance, and above it we constructed a hide from which to look down. I stayed in this man-made nest for seventy-two consecutive hours.

We were unlucky in that the mating season was over and the couple spent perhaps three quarters of their time on a neighbouring perch, watching and waiting. But we could watch their every move unobserved. We could see the way they savaged their newly-emancipated young if they were so precocious as actually to catch a fish; how on the lagoon shore they snatched fish out of the beaks of lesser birds – the grey heron, the little egret, the black heron, which squatted under an umbrella made out of its own plumage. At times the shore resembled a more savage version of an angling competition on the banks of an English river.

And at dawn we could hear the spine-chilling cry of the two birds, and the answering call of the other fish eagles, seeking each other out – the wild cry that travellers have called 'the sound of Africa'.

PART TWO *South West Africa*

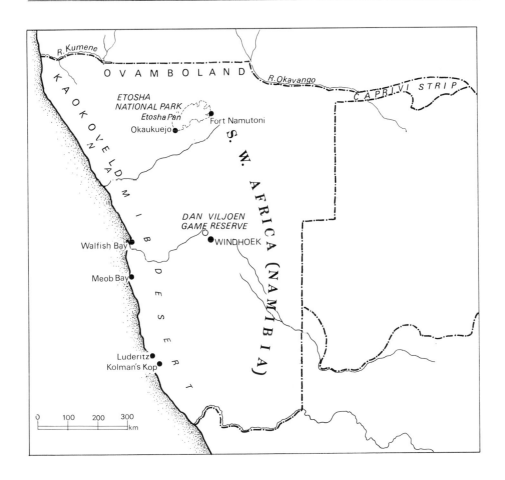

*The Namib Desert: as the heat reaches its
crescendo even the coarse desert grass withers away.*

3 First Catch Your Unicorn

It is difficult for those who have never been there to appreciate either the size, the thinness of population, or the extremes of temperature of Southern Africa. The total area of the British Isles is 94,000 square miles, its population roughly 55,000,000. The area of South West Africa (now Namibia) is nearly four times as great, its population only 574,000. The territory had originally been settled by the Germans in the nineteenth century, but during my stay it was governed by the Republic of South Africa.

Rodney Borland and I came to South West Africa on an early assignment for Anglia. With us on this trip came my wife, Margit – a beautiful young teacher whom I had met and married in Germany. She had left her teaching job to come out to Africa, and she tried hard at first to adapt to the demands of our rigorous outdoor life. She became a very able photographer. But things soon began to go wrong. During my first year with Anglia I was 'on trial', and probably I concentrated more on my work than on Margit. She in turn realized that she wanted to lead a more conventional life. After eighteen months we got divorced and parted as friends.

But that was still in the future when we first arrived in Windhoek, the capital of South West Africa. We found ourselves in luck. An old acquaintance of ours, Bernabe de la Bat, had been appointed Director of Nature Conservation and Tourism for the whole of South West Africa. I went straight to him for permission to film in the wildlife reserves. De la Bat replied that this would take time, as permission had to come from Pretoria; but if I was in a hurry *he* could give me permission to operate on privately owned land, part of which was farmland bordering the Namib Desert. His Capture Officer, Peter Flanagan, was about to go out there and was coming to see him the next day. He would ask him to take us along.

The morning after my arrival Flanagan came into de la Bat's office. He wore – as he almost always wore – a wide-brimmed floppy hat, a green jacket and shorts. My first impression was that he would not be out of place in a Wild West film. He exuded vitality and a raw self-confidence.

On this particular morning de la Bat introduced us and suggested that Flanagan take me as cameraman on his forthcoming 'capture' expedition to the Namib Desert. To say that Flanagan's 'yes' was grudging would be an understatement. He really had no option but to agree, since de la Bat was his superior. He told me later that he had had bad experiences with previous freelance cameramen, who had no idea how rough, tough and dangerous such 'capture' expeditions could be. I was soon to find out.

The object of the operation this time was the magnificent oryx antelope, also known by its Afrikaans name, Gemsbok. The oryx's most striking feature is its long, straight-up pointed horns: it is so familiar in profile to the legendary unicorn that many people believe it is the unicorn's direct descendant. Unlike some breeds of antelope oryx are strong and utterly fearless. They think nothing of attacking a truck; they have been known to turn on a pursuing lion and spear him to death. They are among the few animals – the ostrich is another – who can survive the appalling climate of the Namib Desert. Why not leave them alone? Let me tell you.

This desert is one of the most inhospitable in the world, more hostile even than the nearby Kalahari. It has been built up through the centuries by sands rejected by the Atlantic Ocean. It is composed of huge dunes, constantly shifting to the hissing orders of the ceaseless winds. It can be bitterly cold, but for most of each day it is scorchingly hot. About all that grows there is the coarse desert grass on which the oryx feeds. But as the heat reaches its crescendo in the South African dry season even this grass withers away. The oryx have to seek food elsewhere.

Bordering the desert are huge tracts of farmland on which sheep are pastured. But not just ordinary sheep: the world-famous Karakul sheep, whose pelt is the finest and one of the most highly prized in the world. The pelt is taken from baby Karakuls shortly after birth, when it is at its softest. The starving oryx make their way to the Karakul pastures. But the farmers cannot allow such an invasion of their precious land. This area is not a national park or reserve, so there is nothing to prevent them from killing the oryx as they invade, decimating herd after herd. Hence the operation on which we were now embarked. Flanagan must capture alive as many oryx as possible, in order to transport them to the safe haven of the nearest National Park, so preserving a breed which might otherwise face extinction in this area – the purpose of nature conservation bodies and the World Wildlife Fund in every continent.

The method adopted was at that time unique. Previously attempts had

The oryx antelope and the white lady spider are among the few creatures that can survive the desert's appalling climate.

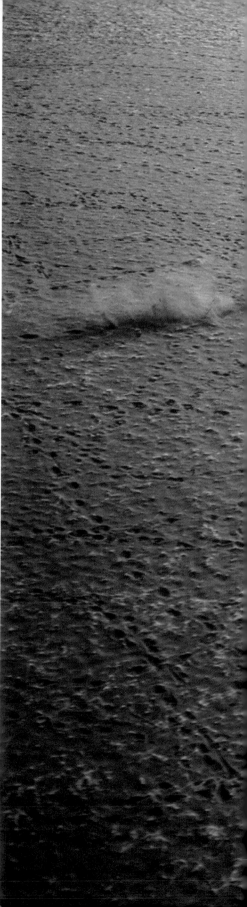

been made to immobilize the animals by firing drugged darts at them. But this failed; the drug worked too slowly, and the oryx vanished into the dunes. The method was known as 'darting'. Flanagan's idea was quite different – to single out of a herd a particular oryx, pursue it in a Land-Rover, station a catcher on the front of the bonnet who would catch it by its tail, then jump off and wrestle with it on the ground. If the catcher missed he usually fell into the soft sand. In any event, catch or miss, the Land-Rover would be travelling at about forty miles an hour. Flanagan made it clear that Rodney and I would have to take our turns on the bonnet. Would we pass the test that the 'sissy' cameramen had failed?

So we set forth in a Land-Rover, six of us. Flanagan at the wheel, Tsotsi, his head boy, on the bonnet, Rodney and I at the back of the vehicle, our cameras set up and at the ready. The crew was completed by Indunwa and Moses, fellow members of Tsotsi's Ovambo tribe. The first tail was successfully caught – Tsotsi was an expert. He jumped down and started to wrestle with the oryx.

'Stay where you are!' shouted Flanagan, and drove straight on in pursuit of another captive. The process was repeated successfully by Indunwa and Moses, each left behind in single combat. Then came Rodney. He was slightly built and his catch was a big bull oryx. Fortunately he was a 'brown belt' at judo; we left him matching skill with strength.

Then it was my turn. With the car still hurtling along at forty miles an hour I scrambled forward on to the bonnet, holding the front rail tightly with my left hand, and succeeded in catching the tail of what seemed to me a very large female. I started to wrestle with her and Flanagan pulled up. For a second I thought he was coming to my assistance. Not at all. He pulled out of his pocket a roll of lavatory paper and strode two hundred yards across the dunes. There he squatted and had a good shit. Just as he returned my oryx broke free. I struggled to keep hold of her, but could not prevent her driving one horn right through one of the Land-Rover's front tyres. Flanagan spent a leisurely twenty minutes mending the puncture, while I held on to my reluctant oryx. Only then did he turn to the task of injecting the animal with the necessary sedative.

We retraced our tracks across the dunes, now dotted with struggling heaps. In due course the four other oryx were successfully sedated and loaded into the jeep. Flanagan told Rodney and me that we had passed the first test. Armed with soap and towel he then marched off into the dunes where his boys had filled a tub with water, and took a bath.

That night, after we had bivouacked, Flanagan showed us another side of his astonishing character. When he had climbed into his sleeping bag he called Tsotsi over and told him to zip it up, which he could perfectly well have done himself.

Then he said, '*Lief ye yo Baas?*' ('Do you love your boss?'), to which Tsotsi ritually replied, '*Ja, Baas*' ('Yes Boss'). It was Flanagan's way of asserting the double relationship of father and son and boss and boy to the 'boy' in whom he had such implicit faith.

It was Flanagan who arranged an archery match between one of his young Ovambos, famed in his tribe for his skill with bow and arrow, and Rodney, himself no mean performer. Here was Rodney, with the upright stance favoured by white men since the days of Robin Hood, and the young Ovambo, crouched in African fashion. To our surprise, and I must admit a measure of relief, Rodney proved the victor. We didn't really want to lose face.

In the following days we captured another thirty-five oryx. After each catch we took them to the *boma,* the reception centre where the animals could recover from the shock of capture and the effect of the drugs used on them, before being released to the safety of the Etosha National Park and the Dan Viljoen Game Reserve.

On the last day our Land-Rover, fully loaded with captured oryx, climbed to the crest of a high sand dune, to be faced by six farmers in a small jeep from a nearby farm, armed with hunting rifles. Their purpose was all too clear: they were poaching. What we knew and they did not was that in the valley behind us was a herd of oryx and springbok. Flanagan got out of the Land-Rover, advanced towards them and demanded to know what they were up to, revealing himself as a Conservation Officer. The leading farmer tried to bluff with some excuses. Flanagan would have none of it and took the number of their car. The farmers refused to give their names or to show their gun licences. By sheer force of personality this intrepid man outfaced them. They gave way, and returned whence they had come. Later they were heavily fined.

When I returned to Windhoek the new car that Anglia had bought for my use had just arrived. It was a Mercedes Unimog. It had four-wheel drive and differential gears designed for cross-country journeys and such high clearance that if you lay on the road reading a book the car could ride over you without touching you. It served us magnificently. Rodney and I nicknamed it Hannibal. In four years we drove Hannibal over fifty thousand miles.

From Windhoek, Rodney and I chartered a plane to do some aerial filming down the coast. Our pilot was an experienced Belgian, Jacques Midgeotte, his plane a Cessna 206. We adapted it for photography by removing its doors.

*Unlike some antelopes oryx are strong
and utterly fearless: they have been known to
turn on a pursuing lion and spear him to death.*

The strip of coastland from Walfish Bay to Luderitz had at the turn of the century been found to be rich in diamond deposits. Now it was dotted with ghost towns. In their frantic rush for riches the miners had stripped each area in turn of its deposits, and then rushed on to the next field, abandoning everything when they left.

Our Belgian pilot had permission to land in this strictly guarded area. Rodney and I had no such thing, but this did not deter us. Over Meob Bay, about a hundred and fifty miles south of Walfish Bay, the engine conveniently 'overheated', so that if necessary we could plead a forced landing. We were unchallenged, and an astonishing sight met our eyes. We found shanty shacks, crammed with tinned food, rotting pieces of furniture and, most startling of all, dozens and dozens of empty champagne bottles. The latter were pockmarked with holes drilled by decades of drifting, gritty sand through even the thick sort of glass that can keep the fizz in champagne for thirty years.

Another ghost town was Kolman's Kop, scene of one of the most spectacular diamond rushes just before the First World War. Here we found the ruins of palatial buildings that might have graced a capital city. There were not only champagne bottles, but even abandoned billiard tables. The whole scene seemed to me a monument to man's greed.

On our way back we passed over other macabre relics of the past.

Dotted here and there, sometimes many miles inland, were rusting shipwrecks, disgorged by the ocean and carried from the coast by the remorseless, ever-shifting sands. This coastline south of Walfish Bay is one of the most treacherous in the whole world.

I was soon called back to Windhoek. Flanagan had now been given the task of rounding up and rescuing as many black-faced impala as possible, and he wanted us to accompany him as cameramen. Black-faced impala are distinguished from other impala by two black streaks down their noses. Their normal pastures were in the Kaokoveld, a tract of near-desert country in the extreme north-west of South West Africa. The few herds that lived here were almost the last remaining of this species.

The main sources of danger to the black-faced impala – apart from animal predators who anyway eat only when hungry and whom the exceptionally swift impala could often evade – were, as with the oryx, cattle and the pastoralists who owned them. The inhabitants of the Kaokoveld belonged to the Ovahimba tribe – one of the most primitive in all Africa. The Ovahimba totally and actively reject civilization in all its forms. For example, when the government bored holes to increase their water supply they deliberately filled them up with rocks. For these Ovahimba, as for most Africans, the sole idea of wealth is cattle, and wealth they literally count by numbers. No matter how scraggy the animals, no matter how diseased, two bad cattle counted more in the eyes of an Ovahimba farmer than the one good beast owned by a neighbour or rival. This primitive method of reckoning wealth was one of the factors that spelt death to the black-faced impala. There simply was not room in the Kaokoveld for both cattle and impala, and the Ovahimbas were seeing to it that it was the impala who suffered.[1]

During the whole of this 'Operation Black-faced Impala' Flanagan was at his most resourceful. He was also at his most eccentric; lesser men might have got into bad trouble for what he did, either with the authorities at Windhoek or with his own native team. For instance, there was the affair of the Winchester cartridges. (These are particularly expensive.) When he reported back to Windhoek after one trip it emerged that he had used 120 of them 'to frighten off elephants'. 'Well,' said de la Bat, 'there must have been a hell of a lot of elephants.' 'Oh,' replied Flanagan airily, 'at least a hundred.' Luckily for him de la Bat had both affection and admiration for this 'lovable rogue'; he at least pretended to believe him. In fact there was not a single elephant in the neighbourhood. The cartridges had been used for target practice.

Under the command once again of Flanagan we set up camp in the heart of the black impala country, just south of the Kunene river which marks the boundary with Angola. In some ways impala presented the same problems as the oryx. Darting would prove ineffective, for they would escape before the drug took effect; daylight pursuit and catching would prove far more difficult, for the impala was a much swifter animal than the oryx. Attempts to net them had proved abortive. The ever-resourceful Flanagan hit upon a new idea. He would literally blind the impala with the dazzling lights of the Land-Rover and hand-held spotlights. The tactics worked beautifully; in a few days we caught 121 impala.

There was an Ovahimba encampment about fifty yards away from ours. One evening the spirit of mischief possessed Flanagan. He turned on, full blast, a tape recording of lions roaring in the jungle. Pandemonium broke out in the native camp. Flanagan made it worse by going out into the bush and blazing away with his gun, screaming wildly. A deputation of Ovahimbas, led by Tsotsi, arrived, pleading for protection. Flanagan explained his practical joke. Tsotsi listened, hesitated, then broke into roars of laughter. No offence was taken. With almost anyone else it would have been.

[1] The African's reckoning of wealth by numbers of cattle owned was and is still gravely affecting the continent's ecology as a simple equation shows. It has been reckoned that it takes two and a half cattle to keep one man alive, but the amount one cow eats is several times the amount that one man consumes.

The next day a group of Ovahimbas was sitting about fifty yards away from our lunch tent. Flanagan asked their leader if they would mind moving as, with the prevailing wind, their smell was overpowering us. The request was granted, and the group moved down-wind of us. A little later a deputation came to say that with the wind now coming from our direction to them, they could not stand our smell and would we move. It was typical of Flanagan that he did not mind in the least.

Flanagan had a gift, amounting to genius, for improvisation in the face of the unexpected. One day the teenage son of the local Ovahimba chief appeared at our camp. He was clearly in pain, and clutching his stomach. He begged us to give him some strong medicine, saying he would die without it. Unfortunately we had been in camp for some considerable time and our medicine chest was practically exhausted. (When word got around that we had medicine all the local tribesmen faked illness just to get hold of some of it.) All we had left were chloroquine tablets. The youth took one, and despite its bitter taste he chewed it with determination.

But it had no effect; the son of a chief needed stronger medicine. Flanagan thought for a while, and played his last card. He reached for a bottle of tabasco sauce, poured out a tablespoonful of it, and told the young African to swallow it very slowly, otherwise it would not work. The youth complied. As it seared first into his gullet, then his stomach, his face contorted into agonized expressions, sweat appeared on his forehead, he started to shake, got up, let out a shriek and vanished into the bush.

I could see Flanagan was really worried, and so were we. Minutes went by. We could be in deadly trouble. An hour later the young man was back, all beaming smiles, bringing with him two goats. He told Flanagan he was completely cured; it was the most powerful medicine in the world. Would Flanagan please accept these goats in exchange for the rest of the bottle? Suppressing both his surprise and his mirth Flanagan accepted them with a good grace.

Overleaf: The giant dunes of the Namib Desert – some fifteen hundred feet high – have been built up over centuries by sand ejected from the Atlantic Ocean.

Following page: Bordering the desert are rich tracts of farmland where precious Karakul sheep are pastured.

One day Rodney and I went with Flanagan and his African helpers to fetch water from the Kunene river. They had been fetching water every day until now, and Rodney and I felt we should take a turn. We also wanted to see the river. We set out in the Unimog soon after breakfast. For about an hour we made our way through wonderful but barren country, meeting here and there odd Ovahimba tribesmen tending their cattle.

When we got to the river we parked the car under some palm trees. Tsotsi and his gang unloaded the buckets and proceeded to fill the forty-four-gallon drums on the back of the Unimog. Rodney, Flanagan, and I went downstream to look at the beautiful Epupa Water Falls, where the Kunene plunged down a deep gorge in its effort to reach the sea. We took a few pictures and ambled back to the vehicle. The men were still busy filling the drums so we decided to walk a little way upstream.

About fifty feet along we came upon a horribly decaying buffalo carcass lying three-quarters hidden in the water. It must have been there for several days. The fast current flowed around it, straight to the place where Tsotsi and his helpers were collecting our drinking water. Rodney and I looked at each other and immediately remembered that the tea in camp had tasted peculiar for the last few days.

I turned round and saw Flanagan coming towards us. I said, 'Pete,

have you always fetched water from this place?' He said: 'Yes, Why?' Then he saw the carcass. I said: 'Don't you think we should pour out all the water and refill the drums further up the river?'

Pete, in his inimitable manner, was silent for a while. Then he pushed his hat to the back of his head, scratched his temple, kicked the carcass, which gave out a hollow sound – as well as a horrible stench – and looked at Rodney and me and said, 'Don't worry about it'. Then he walked away.

That night, once again, we went out catching impala until the early hours. We got up late and had lunch together, and then at about two o'clock in the afternoon we all headed for our tents and camp beds, to prepare ourselves for the next capture session.

There was silence around the camp and only Pete remained sitting next to the trestle table where we had had lunch. Slouched in his seat, with his hat tilted over his face, he was the picture of relaxation. His legs were stretched out under the table. Next to his chair, but just out of reach, was his holster containing his revolver.

I was lying on my camp bed in the shade and had a splendid view of Pete in his chair. He was motionless. Suddenly a fly began to buzz around him. He made a few feeble movements with his hand to chase it off. Then I heard a hissing, blowing sound, which suggested that it had

Leaning from the bonnet of the speeding Land-Rover the catcher had to grab an oryx by its tail and then leap down to wrestle with it.

landed on his face and Pete was trying to blow it away. This proved unsuccessful. I saw his left arm move slowly towards the holster. Stretching out his arm, but without moving the rest of his body at all, he managed to pull his 38 Special Smith and Wesson out of his holster. He placed it in his lap. Then I heard another hissing and blowing sound and saw the large fly settling on the other side of the trestle table.

In slow motion Flanagan picked up the revolver. With the barrel he pushed up his hat. The fly remained on the edge of the table. Slowly Flanagan aimed the revolver, cocked the hammer and fired. The bullet struck the table and splinters flew up in wild profusion. Bottles fell over and smashed to the ground. The barrel was still smoking when he put the revolver on the table. Then he simply pulled his hat back over his eyes and went on sleeping.

Needless to say people came running from every direction shouting 'What happened?' From under his hat Flanagan mumbled: 'Don't worry, I just had some trouble with a fly.'

After we had caught the black-faced impala the problem of what to do with them remained. A reception area had been chosen in the great Etosha National Park near Fort Namutoni, the most picturesque of the tourist camps, but this was nearly three hundred miles away. The South African Air Force came to the rescue by providing a Dakota aircraft. It was a strange airlift. The passengers were sedated black-faced impala – the bucks with the more formidable horns had them sheathed in rubber. The air hostesses were the members of Flanagan's team; Rodney and I were supernumary cargo. We arrived safely at our destination, the reception centre, which consisted of a waterhole surrounded by thick thorn bush walls, where the impala could recover from their fright at capture and the effects of sedation, be examined for disease and finally be set free in the midst of the Etosha National Park.

4 The Drought and the Flood

When Atti Port was sixteen his father took him on a leopard hunt and a leopard jumped him. His father forbade the other members of the party at gunpoint to come to the rescue: Atti must fend for himself. The boy killed the leopard by stabbing him in the belly with his hunting knife. Years later Atti was again jumped by a leopard. This time the leopard pinned him down so that he could not use his knife. As he lay helpless he swore: 'If I survive this, I will never kill another leopard.' A miracle happened: the leopard let him go. From that day on he became an ardent conservationist.

When I first met Atti Port in South West Africa he was capturing leopards and moving them to Etosha. (If leopards were found in private farmland they were usually shot as vermin.) Atti had just developed a new trap which caught the animals without maiming them. I watched him on one occasion dealing with a captured leopard. He opened the trap from behind, grabbed the cat by the tail, and held him in a vice with his feet so that he could inject a tranquillizer into his bottom. With a big strong leopard this was by no means a simple operation.

Rodney and I were with Atti on one occasion when he released a captured leopard and three captured cheetahs into Etosha National Park. He got the necessary veterinary certificates and told me the day for release was at hand.

When I arrived at Atti's farm Rodney had already started to film. Armed with my Arriflex camera I crossed the farmyard where Atti's watchdog, a fearsome beast, lay in his kennel. I reckoned that the chain to which he was tethered could not be more than ten yards long, so I was careful to stay at least that far away from him. I was wrong. The dog shot out of his hut and sank his teeth into my calf. Then, almost as inexplicably as Atti's leopard all those years ago, the dog let go.

I retired hurt, but foolishly tried again. This time I estimated the chain's length at fifteen yards. Once again I was wrong, and suffered for it. Surely it couldn't happen again? The third time I decided to hug the farmyard wall, which was at least twenty-five yards from the dog. Unfortunately the chain was at least twenty-five yards long. On this occasion I had to bang the animal on the head with my camera to make him let go. I escaped, with some nasty gashes in my thigh, to the first-aid of Atti's wife Karin. Antibiotics did the trick, but when I next sallied forth my route was on the far side of the farmyard wall.

As Atti and his helpers coaxed the leopard into the release crate, Rodney and I set up a net inside the cheetah pen. We soon captured the three cheetahs and installed them, together with the leopard, in Atti's truck.

Four hours later we reached the main gate of the Etosha National Park. From there it was only a few miles to Okaukuejo, the Park headquarters. We collected the ranger on duty and went to an open space next to the Etosha Pan where we planned to release the cheetahs. Rodney and I set up our tripods, each equipped with a 12–120 zoom lens. Atti opened the side boards of the truck and the cheetahs were free to leap out. Instead they stood motionless. But Atti was nothing if not inventive. With a stick and a length of rope he managed to pass a noose round one of them and pull it out on to the ground. Meanwhile the ranger grabbed its tail.

A strange scene followed. There is a legend among the farmers and hunters of those parts that if you put butter on the paws of a cat it will never return to the place from whence it came. If this works for a small cat, why should not the same apply to a cheetah? At the worst it could do no harm. Once buttered, the first of our cats took a look around and bounded off into the high grass at the edge of the pan and to freedom, watched curiously by a herd of springbok. Given the same treatment, its fellows followed suit. It was through such releases into the security of Etosha that the cheetah population was enabled to increase.

The leopard was less obliging. We drove, with our Land-Rover and Atti's truck, to the Charitsaub waterhole. There we dumped the crate, leopard and all, on the ground. The truck was reversed towards it, with one of the ranger's sons on the back of it, protected by some strong wire mesh, holding a rope which was connected to the sliding door of the crate. Rodney sat in the truck driver's seat with one camera and I stood outside, thirty yards away, with my tripod. Atti stood about thirty-five

The cheetah alone is fast enough to outpace the graceful springbok. People sometimes ask me 'How can you watch such a grisly spectacle?' But the only difference between us and the predator is that we get someone else to do the job for us.

yards from the crate and clapped his hands to induce the leopard to come out while the sliding door was slowly pulled up.

The leopard charged violently out of the crate and sprang at the wire mesh. Fortunately it did not give way. The sleek cat then instinctively made for the nearest dark place he could find, under the truck.

An extraordinary, and at times very dangerous, game of hide and seek followed. Rodney tried to make the leopard come out by starting the truck's engine. The cat did emerge briefly, but vanished again in between the loading platform and the axle. Rodney drove a few yards and stopped. Slowly the leopard's head appeared right next to the back number plate. Then he came down, stalking along underneath the car, looked at me and vanished into the engine compartment from below.

We could not believe what was happening. I was filming every second. My film eventually ran out, and I changed it as fast as I could, hoping the leopard would stay out of sight until I was ready.

On Atti's instructions Rodney started hooting. Nothing happened. So Atti decided to drive up to the truck in his Land-Rover and open its bonnet. We watched anxiously as the Land-Rover approached. It stopped right in front of the truck and Atti reached out to open the bonnet release catch. The hood swung open and stopped at an angle of about forty-five degrees.

The leopard was lying right on top of the engine. Immediately he crouched, ready to spring. Atti grabbed one of my camera cases and held it up at his open window for protection. No sooner had he done this than the leopard leapt right at the window.

But the beautiful cat was still in no hurry to depart. He climbed back on to the engine and settled down, turning to look at Rodney in the driver's cab only inches away.

Atti began to reverse away in the Land-Rover and suddenly the leopard charged the moving vehicle at full speed, clawing its side. Then he stopped in his tracks, came back to the truck and vanished underneath it. He re-emerged on my side, looked at me, then turned and moved off. Silently I watched and filmed in awe. He slid through the grass and reached the foot of a tree. Like lightning he darted up the trunk and stopped, hidden by the leaves of the topmost branches. A crow which had its nest in the tree hovered above, showering abuse on the unexpected intruder. We all shook our heads in disbelief.

*Cheetahs and leopards found on private farmland
in South West Africa are often shot as vermin.*

The outcome of our day's work was a very popular *Survival* film.[1] It is usually the fate of the television cameraman that, of all the thousands of feet of film he takes, only a minute fraction ever gets shown on the screen. *Cat Out of the Bag* was an exception.

For much of the year the Etosha National Park in South West Africa is almost a desert. Its average rainfall is only 24.6 inches. During the rainy season richness blooms in the land, and the animals can take their fill of it. Then even the barren salt pan in the centre of the reserve yields sustenance and water. But soon it dries up almost completely – providing, incidentally, a trap for the unwary ranger on patrol: for though the pan has a solid and firm crust, almost like a motor-racing track, just below is a quagmire of alkaline mud.

The Etosha National Park used to consist of the whole north-western corner of South West Africa, covering 38,000 square miles. Now, with the Kaokoveld and other regions lopped off, it covers an area of 18,000 square miles, of which a quarter is pan. It still ranks among the great national parks of Africa.

I first visited Etosha when I was a freelancer: I was making films for a local caravan company. This was the first time I met Hymie Ebedes and I took an instant liking to him. Hymie was then, and for many years, chief veterinary officer and biologist for the whole of Etosha. He knew more about animal diseases and ailments than anyone I have known. I remember vividly the first time he asked me to accompany him with my camera. Also in the party was Peter Stark, then one of Etosha's rangers, and later chief ranger of the whole park.

While I was at Okaukuejo, the park headquarters, bushman trackers brought in the news that they had seen a badly injured bull in the Mopani forest some eighty miles away.

Hymie said at once, 'We'll have to dart it.'

'Can I come and photograph it?' I asked.

'Sure, that'll be fine.'

We set forth, the three of us, armed with the necessary equipment plus my camera. We located the elephant near a waterhole. He was obviously in great pain. There was a gaping, festering wound in his left leg. In his present condition he was incapable of charging us. Hymie advanced to within point-blank range, holding a cap-Chur gun with a drugged dart. He fired the dart into the great animal's leg muscle. For a quarter of an

[1]*Cat Out of the Bag,* 1974.

Atti Port invented a box trap, in which the cats could be transported to the safety of Etosha National Park.

hour nothing happened. Then the elephant started to tremble all over, and fell to the ground as if shot.

Hymie rushed forward and started to clean the wound. Even as he did so it looked like a fruitless task. The wound was wide and deep; pus was oozing everywhere. Hymie cleaned it away with antiseptic rags, then covered the wound with the strongest form of antibiotic cream, before plugging it with bandages. It was an eerie scene, the great descendant of the prehistoric mastodon, prostrate, unconscious, and by his side the brilliant veterinary surgeon of the twentieth century.

After half an hour Hymie had finished. It remained only to re-awaken the elephant, which was done by injecting an anti-sedative into a vein in his ear. Within a minute and a half the elephant rose, almost majestically, to his feet and lumbered away into the bush.

For the bushman trackers all this was a miracle. They could understand that you could kill an elephant with a gun, but to 're-awaken him from the dead' – that could only be the work of a great medicine-man.

The brilliant veterinary surgeon of the twentieth century with his giant patient, descendent of the prehistoric mastodon.

Later, the bushmen brought a dead body – one of their tribesmen – to Doctor Ebedes to 're-awaken' him. It took Hymie quite a while to explain to these wonderfully simple people that it was not possible. They went away disillusioned, taking the body with them. Hymie was not such a great medicine-man after all.

Hymie was engaged in a constant warfare against anthrax, a disease fatal to all ruminant animals. Herds of cattle and game of all sorts could be decimated or even wiped out altogether by its onslaught. A dangerous peculiarity of anthrax, which affects Etosha mainly in the rainy season, is the length of time for which the spores remain active. In any carcass that is not wholly burnt they may persist for half a century. Another peculiarity is that established waterholes provide immunity from anthrax, owing to the presence of bacteria in the water.

Obviously, one of the main carriers of the anthrax spores is that scavenger of the African scene, the vulture. Hymie and his colleague Herbert Bourn devised a scheme. Whenever they found an untouched carcass they drugged it. Then they kept watch until the vultures arrived. Very soon these hideous great birds were staggering about like drunken men in the streets of London after a football match. In such a state they were easy to capture. When they were loaded on to our pick-up truck they started to snore in as many keys as the musicologists recognize. When we reached camp the vultures' wings were painted in different colours and little notches were cut into their wing feathers. In this way it was possible to keep track of each bird and test the likelihood of its being a anthrax carrier.

I spent nearly a year in the Etosha Park planning and executing the series of four *Survival* programmes that became known as *The Great Etosha* (1970). Peter Stark was now installed as Chief Ranger in control of the whole park. Peter ranks, in my view, as one of the great men concerned in the conservation of wild life and also one of the most strong-willed and toughest. His iron discipline and will-power were reflected in his steel-blue eyes, which, when he was in earnest, could send shudders down the spine of any would-be adversary.

Before becoming a ranger he had been manager of a cattle ranch that lay adjacent to the boundaries of the park. In that capacity he was credited with having shot fifty-two lions, which had been decimating his cattle, having broken through the wire fencing that guarded the ranch. On one particular occasion he was faced with the problem of a marauding lion which to his knowledge had killed nine of his cattle. It had to be killed, even if it meant pursuing it into the reserve. It did mean just that. He pursued it deep into sacred territory and shot it dead.

The story goes that he was spotted by park rangers. How could he escape? Inspiration came to him. He lay down beside the lion, which had died behind the trunk of a fallen tree. As the rangers approached he lifted the lion's head above the trunk and wagged it. The rangers assumed that the lion was alive, and passed on their way. Stark returned, after a precautionary interval, to his farm.

By the time I met him, however, Peter's reprobate days were over. He was a poacher turned gamekeeper. The farm manager who had broken the laws of the reserve was on his way to becoming its chief warden. He was the finest horseman I have ever met, and his fame as a trainer of horses for what can only be called bush warfare was legendary. He spent countless hours getting from them absolute obedience and dispelling their natural fears while facing elephants, so that they became successful herders of these huge animals which created havoc on farms bordering the reserve. He used horses too to follow the tracks of poachers. His services to the cause of conservation, once he had become an employee of the Etosha National Park, were immense.

Peter had one weakness – for honey. Whenever, on his patrols through the reserve, he came upon a beehive in a tree he removed half of it, heedless of the number of stings he received. Half of the honey comb he left untouched, in order, as he put it, not to discourage the bees too much. Then he marked the tree. In due course he had blazed a regular honey trail through the park.

In the months following the rains the wild animals of Etosha suddenly seemed to multiply. Rivers that in the dry season simply did not exist flooded the pan so that it resembled a great lake; the desert around it bloomed and the animals appeared, from the elephant and lion to zebra, ostrich and flamingoes. But in the year that I was there the flamingoes were struck by a terrible disaster.

The Etosha salt pan is one of the great meeting places of the African flamingo. From far and wide the birds come to build their nests and hatch their eggs in its short-lived shallow waters. Normally, by the time the pan dries up the chicks are ready to fly and fend for themselves. But on this occasion abnormal wind conditions upset nature's plans. The pan dried up much earlier than usual. Father and mother flamingoes were forced to seek food elsewhere and abandon thousands of chicks to their fate.

The impending disaster was first revealed by a tourist who chanced to meet a young flamingo staggering along a track. The Etosha rangers

To the amazement of the bushman trackers,
the stricken elephant 'reawoke from the dead'.

*Peter Stark trained his horses to overcome their
natural fear of elephants so that they could
drive the runaway herds back into the park.*

were alerted. Aerial reconnaissance revealed the extent of the damage.
Empty nests lay scattered across the landscape, and hundreds of young
birds were trapped in the mud. This was a serious handicap to the rescue
work. If the starving birds could be transported to the waters of a nearby
lagoon called Fisher's Pan – the only stretch of water that had not yet
dried up – many of them might be saved. But the thick, oozing mud just
below the pan's hard crust made it difficult for the rescue trucks to
navigate it.

Nevertheless the dedicated park rangers somehow achieved what
looked like the impossible. The flamingoes were brought safely to the
lagoon, where nutrients were added to the water. It was estimated that
30,000 flamingoes were saved. The whole operation was a major feat of
conservation.

One day when I was at Etosha three bushmen reported to Peter Stark
the presence of a marauding lion. Peter and I found lion tracks on a
muddy road bordering the park, leading from a hole in the wire fencing.

He was, we discovered, hunting outside the park by night and returning to his proper place by day. Peter was reluctant to kill him – after all he was a park lion. He decided to try to warn him off. To that end, he removed the bullets from a 12-bore shotgun and substituted pellets made of rock salt crystals.

'I'm not going to dart him,' he said, 'he wouldn't know anything about that. I must teach him a lesson. These pellets will hurt, but they won't kill him.'

We started to track the lion, and soon came across a newly killed cow. A little later we found the lion, and the lesson was duly administered. The lion gave a great roar and bounded off into the bush. The local farmers were furious that Peter had not killed the beast, and with some justification, from their point of view: for the very next night the lion returned and killed three cattle. The farmers' patience was finally exhausted, and they took matters into their own hands. They poisoned a partly eaten carcass with strychnine. When Peter tracked down the lion he was dead, having died in extreme agony. All around him bushes and scrub were torn up by their roots. On examining the body Peter found one side riddled with the rock salt pellets. The lesson had not been severe enough.

Another of Peter Stark's problems at Etosha was runaway elephants. Before the park had been enclosed elephant migration trails used to run across the neighbouring farmlands; and an elephant never forgets.

One day Peter heard that a herd of elephants had broken out and was creating havoc on a farm called Onguma. He took a walkie-talkie radio, so that he could communicate with Rodney and me while we patrolled the road outside the fence in our Unimog. Peter singled out four big bulls and drove them back, using horses, pistol shots, and the clamour of the bushmen riders. The bulls emerged on to the road at a fast walk – the greatest speed elephants normally manage. We were well positioned, about seventy-five yards away, thanks to the radio contact. The elephants crashed through the strong wire fence as if it were matchwood and were safely back in the reserve, while I had achieved the key shot around which to build a film.

Wherever the borders of civilization are extended by man, wildlife is on the retreat; there is less and less land to go round. This is true even in a vast country like South West Africa. One of the species particularly at risk here was the roan antelope.

Until recently the roan – one of the strongest and largest of all antelopes – occurred in large numbers throughout the country; but now a count revealed that only about four hundred animals were left.

The surviving animals were in the extreme north-west of the country, next to the Botswana border. They were about two hundred miles from the nearest town – and yet they were still at the mercy of man the predator. For this was bushman country; and the roan antelope was the bushmen's natural food. These primitive people were ignorant, of course, of ecological problems. If nothing was done the roan would soon become extinct in South West Africa.

In order to save the species, the Department of Nature Conservation launched the most costly single game rescue operation ever attempted in Southern Africa. The object was to capture the roan and bring them to Etosha National Park, where they had once been plentiful and where they would be safe from hunting and poaching. But to get them there was a problem. The distance to Etosha was six hundred miles; much of the road was soft sand and could only be negotiated in four-wheel-drive vehicles. The other alternative was to transport them by air. There were doubts about this, but the department sent an experienced pilot on an aerial survey of the roan antelope habitat to look for a place where a four-engined Lockheed Hercules aircraft could land. After much reconnaisance an airstrip was chosen: the dried-up bed of the Khaudum River.

A month before the scheduled flight five white and fifteen black rangers assembled together with us, the *Survival* team, to catch the roan. The Capture Officer, 'Dupe' Du Plessis, and his colleague, the splendid veterinary surgeon Dr Ian Hofmeyr, in overall charge, decided to place their camp very close to the capture area – a comparatively small tract of bush not more than a few miles in circumference, adjacent to the dry river bed. They then called in a helicopter, which, flying or hovering overhead, would dart the antelope, leaving them to be picked up by following trucks.

The seating area in a helicopter is pretty small. There was no question of cramping it further by adding my two hundred pounds of weight. Luckily I got permission from its admirable pilot, David Todd, an ex-RAF Squadron Leader, to install my camera by tying it to the middle seat. It was controlled by a switch on the pilot's joystick. I marked the exact area which any photograph would cover on the perspex glass, known to helicopter fliers as 'the bubble'. Then I left it all to David. Ian Hofmeyr sat in the passenger seat with his dart-gun, and communicated with the vehicles on the ground by walkie-talkie.

Darting roan antelopes from a helicopter is very difficult. They are cunning creatures. As soon as they heard the helicopter they fled into the trees on the riverbank. Several times the helicopter brushed the topmost branches of the trees in order to dislodge them. This meant filming was going to be difficult. The chopper had to hover within fifty feet of the animals in order to get a successful shot. But David Todd performed miracles with his machine. When a darted roan went down one of the following vehicles was called by radio and guided to the spot where the antelope was to be picked up. Then it was driven back to the *boma*.

I had helped the capture team to set up a reception *boma* made of nylon mesh. Unfortunately the first roan antelope to enter found they could easily get out. So we tried lining the nylon mesh with white plastic sheeting: and the antelope obliged by thinking they were surrounded by a high wall. In a few days seventy-four roan were safely inside.

On the appointed day the Lockheed Hercules arrived to collect them. The pilot faced a formidable task, manoeuvring the aircraft along the narrow stony riverbed; but putting on a full throttle thrust for the reverse propellors, he managed to land it brilliantly. After loading he lifted off with fifty yards to spare, and the plane vanished in a cloud of dust. Seventy-four roan antelopes were on their way to a new life in Etosha National Park.

During the year in which I made my headquarters at Etosha, Hymie
Ebedes got wind of a plan to create a game-proof fence along the park's
northern edge, adjacent to the border with Ovamboland. The intention
was to stop the wild animals wandering north, particularly into the
Ovambo farmlands. But Hymie had heard that the fence could cut across
the northern tip of Etosha Pan, and he was worried that this might
disrupt the circular migration movement of animals, in particular the
zebra. He formed a plan. How he put it into practice is shown in my film
Striped Horse with a Red Collar (1970).

Hymie's idea was to keep track of young female zebras. Zebras live
and move in small family units – a few females with their young, some
sub-adult males, all led by a dominant male. Often the latter is chal-
lenged for leadership by a younger male from another unit. I have seen
them locked in bitter struggles, and frequently the younger stallion
prevails.

In his Land-Rover Hymie moved up on a female with her foal. When
she started to run Hymie darted her, then watched until she started
swaying and collapsed. The foal immediately started nuzzling her and
the stallion stood by; but when Hymie approached, they moved off to
watch from a distance.

Hymie produced a red collar with a yellow number on it. He used

bolts to clamp the collar around the zebra's neck and as weights to keep the number upright. He tested the animal for heartbeat and respiration, then gave her the necessary antidote to bring her round. Watching from a distance he saw the stallion cautiously approaching as the mare made her first groggy movements. As soon as he saw the red collar he jumped, retreated and then stared intently. The family remained watching. The mare recovered quickly, shaking her head from time to time to rid herself of the unexpected collar. Presently the stallion plucked up courage to approach Red Collar, and the family moved off.

In all I photographed Hymie putting collars around seven zebras' necks. All were watched through the year. I myself found zebra number twenty at various places in sequence round the pan. The family to which she belonged ended up at the western end of the pan, where it had started. Hymie had proved his point. The zebras were practising seasonal rotation of pastures round the pan so that the areas they visited were never overgrazed. But if a fence were to be erected across the northern parts of the pan, the zebra would, as it were, be forced off course, and ecology could suffer.

The zebra naturally suffers from predators, particularly lions. It suffers even more from poachers. But why principally do poachers poach? The reason lies in the great cities of the so-called civilized world, in places

Zebra follow a fixed migration route around the Etosha pan, so that their pastures are never over-grazed.

where fashion prevails: in London, Paris, New York, San Francisco, Tokyo. A zebra skin is a lovely thing, much prized when made up into a coat or hung on a wall. Does a rich tourist who buys a zebra skin in, say. Nairobi, realize that she (or he) is signing the death warrant of at least one, probably more, zebras? For the shop will undoubtedly replace the skin with another.

The sale of zebra and leopard skins, not to mention elephants' tusks, is reaching enormous proportions. The enemies of conservators are just as much the souvenir-hunting tourists and furriers of the world as the poachers who are their initial suppliers. We as educated people should know better. Wildlife is a treasure to any country, one of the few replenishable resources left in the world. Recently I saw a young woman join a tourist group that was setting out for a 'hide' to see a leopard on its kill. She was wearing a leopard–skin coat. I was not amused.

5 Lions at Etosha

Evening after evening, as the orange globe of the sun sinks rapidly in the west, clouds of dust move rapidly down the road that leads to Okaukuejo. It is an inflexible rule at Okaukuejo, the 'capital' of the Etosha National Park, that all tourists must be within the camp perimeter by sunset. Probably the drivers mean to be back in good time, but the temptation to turn aside when you spot a lion kill can be irresistible. Often, therefore, as night begins to fall, there is a mad scramble to reach the gate; and the tourists in all but the leading car arrive like bags of flour, choking and spluttering out the white Etosha dust, but safe for the night.

I was more fortunate. Bernabe de la Bat had given me and my new assistant, Lee Lyon, permission to leave the road and stay out all night. Lee was a tall attractive girl, with an incredible determination to succeed not only in photography but later also in filming. She had blossomed in the sunny world of California, then worked with Des Bartlett in Jackson Hole, Wyoming, and later on his Baja film. She was strong-willed, a talented photographer, and she loved animals and had a deep understanding for them; she was just the partner I needed. We were very close during the three years we spent together. Unfortunately our friendship never matured into something more – as I, and I think she, had hoped. I suppose we were just too independent. It was a sad moment for me when, years later, we parted.

Lee and I now had the chance, if we could find them, of following a pride of lions all through a pale, moonlit tropic night. With this in view *Survival* Anglia had invested in an image intensifier which enabled us to film in the dark, though only in monochrome, and had equipped our Haflinger four-wheel-drive vehicle with bunks so that we could take it in turns to sleep. The camera was put on a special tripod and with the aid of a quick-change plate could be removed or put into position within seconds.

We made our way one evening to a waterhole, and settled down to wait. At first we heard only the sounds of the African night: a barn owl was hooting, and a hyena called in the east. Later six jackals came down to the water to drink. The wind dropped, and the creaking of the wind-pump which fed the waterhole stopped. I kept watch while Lee slept. Then suddenly I saw a shape moving; the silence suggested a large cat. I pulled up my binoculars and strained to focus. I glanced at my watch; it was one-twenty.

One after another the big cats approached without a sound. The lioness in the lead was about fifteen yards away now. I woke Lee and she came to the window. The lioness made straight for the car, stopped about three feet from it, and slowly sat on her haunches. We kept absolutely still: we could hear the lioness breathing. The tension was almost unbearable. After facing the great cat for quite a while the human Lyon lost her nerve and slowly slid below the window. The lioness moved to the left and headed for a large acacia tree.

There were now six lions: one big male, two large females, and three sub-adults. They all went to the tree and clawed it deeply. The large male then turned around and moved slowly towards the waterhole. At its edge he stopped, looking at his own reflection. His mouth touched the water, sending ripples across the mirror-like surface. Frogs lining the banks dived for safety. Approaching in the distance were more lions: two sub-adults, and three cubs playfully chasing and stalking, then charging and clawing each other. More and more lions arrived until we counted about fourteen. Then abruptly, almost as if by command, they all disappeared to the west. Only the three sub-adults remained silent and motionless.

Against the darkness of the sky I could make out the silhouette of a giraffe approaching quietly and carefully, its hooves moving the odd rock in the process. There was no wind, but she seemed to sense something was amiss and she was on her guard. Maybe it was us. The sub-adults, watching her, went into a crouching position. One vanished behind a bush whilst the others stalked very slowly toward the giraffe, their muscles rippling in the pale light. Since they were only sub-adults I doubted very much whether they would actually attack her. But the temptation at least to chase was too much to resist.

Step by step the giraffe approached, her head turning nervously with ears erect to catch any sound or scent of danger. One of the sub-adults crouched, the point of his tail flicking from right to left to right, his head pressed to the ground, his feline body tensed like sprung steel. Suddenly he launched into a lightning charge, but the distance was still too great, and the giraffe took off, leaving three disappointed lions behind. These errors of judgement will continue for some time but one day their stalks will be as deadly as a bullet.

*Lee loved animals and had a deep understanding
of them: she was just the partner I needed.*

Fifteen minutes later all the lions came back, as if they had deliberately moved away to give the youngsters a chance. Again they drank at the waterhole, and then all except the large male were swallowed by the night. We started the engine. Immediately the large male's head turned towards us, and he rose from the grass. I sensed that he was going to charge. His massive body came at us at terrifying speed, to ward us off from the pride. Then, growling and with his tail erect, he retreated and lay under a tree eyeing us, obviously agitated.

He got up and went to a thorn bush, turned around and marked the bush by lifting his tail and spraying a mixture of urine and scent over the leaves. (This indicates to other males that the territory is occupied, and also how recently the owner has passed.) Then he followed the rest of the pride.

*Anglia invested in an image intensifier which
enabled us to film in the dark.*

We went after them and soon found all fourteen lions moving slowly
across the plain. Most of them, including the young and the males,
gradually fell back. Only three females moved on, and we followed
them. One stopped and all three crouched. Nervously we scanned the
horizon. Moving slightly further on we could see three oryx looking at
us in the sparse moonlight. We were probably diverting their attention
from the real danger, for their heads were turned in our direction. As we
watched one lioness pushed herself inch by inch through the grass to get
a good vantage point for a full charge. Somehow, subconsciously, our
predatory instinct came to the fore. Our hearts raced: will she succeed?

All three oryx broke into a gallop. The closest one was just a bit too
slow: the lioness charged and hit the prey with full force. She turned a
somersault with the oryx's neck in her mouth, then the other two
lionesses moved in. Triumphant and exhausted the successful female
stood over the carcass, her mouth drenched and reddened with blood.
They all turned and looked in our direction, their mouths blowing steam
in the coolness of the night. Our heartbeats slowed: the hunter had won.

The other lions approached at a canter and joined in an incredible feeding frenzy, growling and clawing. Jackals arrived almost instantly, howling their long eerie call and adding to the drama of the night. This suggested that the pride was accompanied by jackals throughout their wanderings. The older female who had done the killing lay down next to the feeders, seemingly disgusted at their behaviour. Suddenly the two big males appeared like shadows in the night, forcing and bullying their way to a good feeding position. We heard painful cries as the sub-adults and cubs got pushed aside by the adults. More and more of the adult females dropped out until only the young and the big males remained. They all roared twice in concert, and the sound rolled like thunder over the plains of Etosha.

People sometimes ask me: 'Why don't you interfere? How can you watch such a grisly spectacle? It is awful how these animals kill!' Then I ask: 'Do you eat meat?' Usually the answer is 'Yes'. 'Well, the only difference between us and the predator is that we get somebody else to do the job for us.' Many people reply that humans kill humanely. Which is of course untrue: animals led to slaughter in an abbatoir seem to sense their imminent death. A prey animal does not sense doom and usually death comes fast. I am convinced, too, that animals have a built-in 'shock safety valve'. I have seen young lions pull down a young impala that was very much alive without the buck uttering a sound, its eyes staring with shock.

We followed our pride for several days; they seemed unconcerned at our filming. Then we lost them. Thinking it was a likely rendezvous we returned to another Etosha waterhole called Gemsbokvlakte. When we got there Lee lit the gas cooker and started to make a meat stew with onions. The sky turned yellow and the disc of the sun sank rapidly in the west. Out of the bush came a giant bull elephant, heading for the waterhole. We were almost in his path. About fifty yards from us he stopped and held up his trunk like a periscope. The smell of the onions must have attracted him. At least that was what Lee thought, for she quickly turned off the cooker. The elephant came right up to the car in which we were sitting, and poked his trunk through one of the camera apertures, waving it about within inches of my face. I was actually more surprised than frightened.

He could have destroyed the car with a single swipe. But after a while he removed his trunk, trumpeted to his four fellow bulls, who in the meantime appeared to have surrounded the vehicle, and led them off towards the waterhole. Soon they had their fill, the sun was gone and they moved off slowly like shadows in the night. Lee and I re-heated the onion stew and consumed it thankfully.

On another evening at Gemsbokvlakte we spotted some jackals lurking beneath the bushes, apparently waiting for the lions to vacate a carcass. It is a good maxim that where there are jackals lions won't be far away, and sure enough we soon espied a huge male lion standing over the remains of a carcass. The lion looked at us, his face scarred by untold battles. He came towards the car and lay down under a bush. The jackals immediately moved in on the carcass and grabbed a few bites.

Suddenly all we could see was a yellow-brown flash through the thorn bushes and a lioness came charging out at full speed. The last jackal only just managed to get away in time. The large male immediately roared as if to applaud. The female then lay down on her side under a bush well within sight of the carcass and fifteen yards from our car, uttering what seemed like a sigh of relief. Peace and quietness prevailed.

Three hours later the dry brown grass parted and a six-months-old cub appeared. He glanced at us and moved up to the carcass. Another cub emerged, went up to the large female and pawed her, indicating that he wanted to nurse. The running noise of the camera did not seem to worry them, and I was able to get a close-up of the little cub's face suckling. It was a picture of total contentment. We were so intent on capturing this memorable moment on film that we did not notice two more cubs coming out of the bush. They too began to suckle, while the first to appear stuck to the remains of the carcass, successfully holding a few eager jackals at bay. When they had had their fill the female got up, stretched and yawned. The first light appeared; it was six-thirty. She moved off and the cubs followed her, crouching behind a cluster of grass and finally pouncing upon her in a mock-charge. She called gently to the cubs, who followed her into the bushes.

We heard a lion roaring in the south. All the members of our pride got up and moved towards the waterhole. Just as the female arrived at the water a large male we had not seen before came running after her and attacked her, clawing her and baring his teeth. She lay down in a submissive posture, but soon jumped up and sunk her fangs into the lion's hide. Then she roared to summon her own male, whose appearance from behind some thorn bushes put an end to the fight. The strange male lay down and the female joined her cubs at the water, licking and grooming them. She took a long drink.

After a time the strange male again attacked the lioness, and a vicious, snarling fight ensued, hair flying and dust swirling. The strange male lay down and the two males snarled at each other at a distance of about fifty yards. The female returned to the cubs, licking and grooming them. Occasionally she snarled at the strange male. Then they all lay down quite calmly. In the distance a herd of zebra appeared, ears erect, alerted

For some reason the strange male won the day.

by the sounds of battle. Suddenly the female got up, nuzzled up to the strange male and moved off with him. There was no more antagonism: for some reason the new male had won the day.

During all this time the cubs played happily with one another, hiding behind rocks, pouncing and charging in clouds of white alkaline dust.

Again the female roared – at first a moan, then a few full-throated roars which slowly ebbed away into several successive grunts, causing temporary panic in a nearby zebra family group. Then she moved off with the new male. The old male roared as the two vanished in the bushes. He followed them along the road to the south where he marked several bushes. The three cubs were now alone; but they carried on playing – climbing trees, clawing the bark, chasing terrified blacksmith plovers and black koorhahns.

Abruptly they stopped and waited in the grass. A zebra came past as well as some springbok, one of which almost bumped into a cub hiding behind a rock. I am not sure which was more frightened, the cub or the springbok. With a warning snort the cub ran away and then came back to have another look. A lark, which was not amused when one of the cubs moved into his territory, got up and dive-bombed the startled creature, whose expression grew more and more amazed as the brave little bird continued his attack. The cubs moved on until they reached a dense cluster of bushes. A female black-bellied koorhahn shot out of the thicket, showering abuse at the little intruders. They sniffed the place carefully and hid behind the thick grass. It looked as if this was one of their regular hiding places. Just as the last cub vanished the camera ran out of film. It was nine o'clock now, and the sound of tourist cars began to break the silence.

My experiences of following lions at Etosha gave me the idea of making a film centred around one of the park's waterholes.[1] It turned out to be my favourite of all the half-hour films I have made. The very essence of African wildlife seems to be concentrated in it.

Lee and I spent four months making the film, and then compressed it into what ideally could happen in a single day at one of Etosha's waterholes.

First, at about seven o'clock, a covey of guinea fowl come for what might be called their early morning cup of tea. Then as the light grows stronger, the red hartebeeste, first of the antelopes, arrives, soon to be jostled at the waterhole's edge by a herd of zebras, and then springbok. As Lee and I watch and photograph from our hides a Kori-bustard arrives from the sky, and presently that wondrous bird the ostrich, and the mongoose, terror of snakes.

Soon a pride of lions arrives, arousing acute neuroses in most of the other animals (the graceful koodoo takes flight), but particularly among the zebras, the lions' most regular prey. Soon the lions have the waterhole more or less to themselves, for though the other animals know that lions usually kill only in the evening or at night, one can never tell. Only the

---

[1] *Twelve Hours at the Waterhole*, 1975.

The lioness' mate lay and snarled in the distance.

elephant is immune from fear as he surges towards his drink in stately manner, but the gloriously ugly warthog is wary.

A young lioness decides to play a game of 'stalk the zebra'. She is too well fed from last night's kill to want to kill again, but she starts to crouch and look fierce. The zebras, the hartebeests, the gemsbok and other antelopes scatter in alarm. The lioness desists; she has had her fun. Among the other morning drinkers is the fascinating giraffe, acrobatically lowering its neck and spreading its legs so that its mouth can drink.

Meanwhile it is playtime for most of the animals, playtime that sometimes proves rough. Two zebra stallions go at it hammer and tongs. Then they begin to wilt in the blazing, dust-ridden heat of noon. They and the other animals seek shade wherever they can find it. The waterhole is deserted.

Interest revives in late afternoon. The animals have to drink, but now most of them know that they do so at their peril: even this early the pride of lions might be waiting in ambush. Heads turn nervously, ears prick. A family of zebras suddenly makes off in what proves unnecessary panic. The lions are biding their time until darkness falls – a darkness filled with the howling of hyenas, the crying of jackals, the trumpeting of elephants, the satisfied roar of a lion that has already made its kill and is sharing it with his family. The twelve daylight hours at the waterhole are over.

As the light grew stronger a herd of zebras came to jostle
for a space at the waterhole. Among the other morning drinkers
was the fantastic giraffe.

Elephants at Etosha.

PART THREE   *Ethiopia*

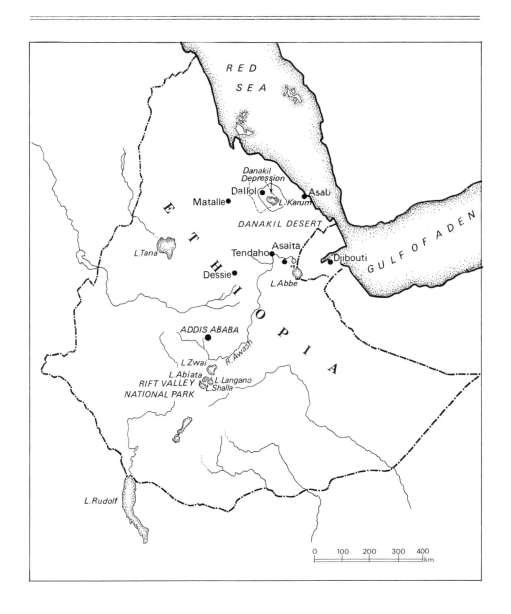

6 The Lion of Judah

I had always wanted to go to Ethiopia, and on one occasion while I was in London, watching rushes of the material I had sent home, Colin Willock called me into his office and told me there was a possibility of making two one-hour films there. The first would be about the pelicans' breeding colony on Lake Shala[1], the other about the Danakil desert and its savage people. I needed no further incentive; but I had one. Colin told me that one of my companions at Lake Shala would be Leslie Brown, which delighted me.

I was met on arrival at Addis Ababa by Emil Urban, the Professor of Zoology at Addis Ababa University, who together with Leslie Brown had already conducted a survey of the white pelicans of Lake Shala. In his quiet way, he was, with his knowledge and imperturbability, as welcome a colleague as Leslie Brown, who arrived the next morning. Leslie and I then proceeded to Lake Langano.

Langano, Abiata and Shala – these are the three lakes in the great Rift Valley of Ethiopia with which the pelican story is concerned. In the middle of the lovely Lake Shala is Pelican Island, where the pelicans, countless numbers of them, come to live and nest.

The reason for this is simple. Lake Shala is up to eight hundred feet deep, more than one hundred square miles in area, strongly alkaline and devoid of fish. Hence no fishermen, no activity, no human noises, nothing to disturb the pelicans. It is their perfect home and breeding ground.

---

[1] *Pelican Flyway*, 1971.

*Lake Shala is the perfect breeding ground
for the great white pelican.*

But there was one snag. If there were no fish, how could they eat? Only four miles away lay Lake Abiata. This shallow lake, also alkaline, is fed by two fresh-water streams. It teems with algae, on which great shoals of fish can feed. Between the two lakes, however, there is a range of mountains fifteen hundred feet high, over which the pelicans had to fly.

How did they get over the mountains? Leslie Brown explained. Every morning a thermal airstream – a current of hot air – rises from the mountain shore opposite. Punctually at ten o'clock each morning the pelicans set off from Shala, flying low over the lake, then catching one of the thermals which carries them over the mountain ridge between the two lakes. They plane down to alight on Lake Abiata, where they fish and fish and fish. They stay the night, then, lifted up on another airstream, they return to Shala loaded with food supplies.

I filmed the whole operation. It meant climbing fifteen hundred feet of precipitous mountain with my tripod and eighty pounds of equipment on my back, starting at dawn to get a head start on the pelicans.

For a few days I reconnoitred the area with Leslie, deciding on places to set up hides. Then Emil and his assistant Tim Jefford joined us, bringing with them their speedboat from which I saw not only Shala but two other small islands which Leslie and Emil had christened Abdim and Cormorant. Leslie and I started to navigate the treacherous waters of Lake Shala in the tiny little aluminium boat with a ten horse-power engine which we had borrowed from the Game Department. A strong wind sprang up, covering the lake in foot-high waves. It was a miracle that in our tiny craft we ever made the shore. I returned at once to Addis Ababa, where I telephoned Aubrey Buxton, explained the situation and got permission to buy a fifty horse-power engine and a rubber dinghy. Now I could really get to work.

In my hide on Lake Shala I watched and filmed for the next few weeks. Often there were as many as three thousand pelicans on this tiny island. I shot a great deal of film: but still was not satisfied. If only I could get closer to the birds!

Then one day when we were visiting Emil Urban in Addis Ababa I had a brilliant idea. In a local museum we found a broken stuffed pelican, which we bought for a song. Take the stuffing out, mend the broken head, make room for my head and the camera where the stuffing had been, place the contraption on a float, which would then look like a pelican. Thus disguised I could swim right among the pelicans.

This stratagem worked, and for days, to my intense pleasure, I could swim among groups of pelicans, photographing their every activity. It worked so well, in fact, that one day, when I returned to the shore and

A stuffed pelican found in an Addis Ababa museum provided me with an excellent disguise.

took off my pelican head, I found that I had been followed by a baby pelican which obviously thought I was its mother. It stayed with the beached dummy bird all night. Only in the morning did it return to its rightful parent.

While I was filming the pelicans at Lake Shala Colin Willock and his wife Joan came to visit me. Colin had come, as he so often did, to see for himself. This habit was one of his most valuable qualities: it gave the *Survival* cameramen confidence in the end product that would come out of their work. The words 'Written by Colin Willock' appearing in a film's credits were a guarantee of merit.

Overleaf: Two breeding pairs of pelicans known to scientists as 'knobbers'.

I went to Addis Ababa to meet Colin and Joan, and we checked in at the Ghion Hotel. That evening as we were having dinner at a Chinese restaurant just round the corner we suddenly heard the siren of a fire engine. It was followed soon after by a second. I said jokingly, 'I expect the hotel is on fire'.

By the time we had ordered our dinner and the waiter had asked what we would like to drink, a third fire engine came down the road, but this time I noticed his indicator flashing – he was going to turn towards our hotel. Just at that moment the owner of the restaurant remarked casually to a passing waiter that the Ghion Hotel was on fire. This statement catapulted us into action. All of my equipment was in my room, and it was not insured. Racing for the door we explained to the manager that we were sorry to have to rush off, but we would see him again another night.

As we ran up the road we could see above the trees the orange glow and the intense smoke of a fiercely burning fire. The road leading up to the hotel was already blocked by the soldiers, who had orders not to let anyone pass. It took quite a while to convince the officer that we were guests at the hotel, and desperate to get back in order to see which part of the hotel was in flames. When he arrived we saw thankfully that it was not the wing we were staying in.

Firemen were busy rolling the hoses to a large swimming pool to connect them to the pumps on the trucks. On the roof of one fire engine a fireman held the nozzle of the hose, bracing himself in expectation of the enormous pressure of water which was about to come out. The engine revved, but all that came out was about a pint of water splashing to the ground.

In the meantime another fireman had drawn his revolver and started firing holes into the windows in order to get water into the burning rooms. The firemen were frantically working to get the pump going. One appeared on a nearby roof with a large axe, trying to smash the windows. Suddenly the pump started working, and the powerful burst of water wiped him clean off the roof. By then three fire engines were going and literally half the swimming pool emptied into the building

Previous page: At ten o'clock each morning
the pelicans set off to catch a thermal airstream
to go fishing at Lake Abiata.

Left: A female shades her chick during the hot hours
of the day while her mate is at Lake Abiata. The
parent birds take it in turns to do the fishing.

to extinguish the fire. We went back to the restaurant feeling enormously relieved.

The next day we went to Lake Shala. Colin was mesmerized by its strange beauty. In order to accommodate the visitors I moved out of my tent and slept naked under a mosquito net. Next morning I woke up covered from head to foot in ticks. I had been sleeping on ground recently abandoned by the pelicans, on whom ticks delight to feed. Failing pelicans they had settled on me. I spend most of that morning in a state of violent itch, picking them off.

The story of Pelican Island did not end when our film was complete. Soon afterwards we heard that the Emperor Haile Selassie wished to see it.

On the appointed evening Emil and I presented ourselves at the Jubilee Palace. The drive was lined by the Emperor's bodyguard. The palace entrance was a great glass door, and inside we saw a huge, red-carpeted branching staircase, each branch ending on a first floor balcony. Brilliant chandeliers lit the scene. It was like a fairy-tale castle.

Emil and I were ushered into a small room where we were introduced by the Lord Chamberlain to the whole Cabinet.

Then a liveried steward entered, struck the floor with his gold-topped stick, and announced, 'His Imperial Majesty, the Emperor'. We filed out and stood at the foot of the staircase. Haile Selassie appeared on the balcony above. Slowly he descended, preceded by a little Chihuahua dog. At the foot of the staircase members of his family knelt and kissed the ground. (I had been told that as a foreigner I need only give a modest bow.)

I was introduced to the Emperor. He was a tiny little man, aging now, but he had a regal presence. He welcomed us warmly and led us all down to the cinema in the basement. On the way I was told by an official that it might not be possible to show the whole of my film, as the Emperor also wanted to see a new magician who was currently the rage of Addis Ababa.

Now if there is one thing I am allergic to it is magicians who saw people apart. They induce in me an actual physical nausea. Particularly this magician, who began by piercing his neck with stilettos, then sawed through a girl in a box, then did the same with a man, and so on. All I could do was to keep my head bowed low, and pretend that I was having constantly to tie up my shoelaces. The magician went on for an hour and a half. After this I was told that the Emperor was tired and would I please keep my film showing to half an hour. I did however manage later, after the Emperor had gone to bed, to show the whole film to the Cabinet.

The film – or what he saw of it – must have impressed Haile Selassie, for afterwards he announced his intention of visiting Lake Abiata and Lake Shala to see the pelicans for himself. The Ethiopian Game Department began making preparations for the visit. Emil had, however, considerable experience of organization carried out by Ethiopians. He had misgivings, and prepared alternative plans. He persuaded a number of English friends to lend him their boats – just in case. A small flotilla was assembled, including a Boston Whaler with an eighty horse-power engine. It was just as well, for on the day before the projected visit a message came to Emil from the Game Department: 'Please organize boats at Abiata'.

On the great day the Imperial procession arrived. First came a truck with Haile Selassie's plain-clothes bodyguard, then a Land-Rover with the special bodyguards. Last an American car called a Willy's Wagoneer arrived, flying the Emperor's flag and bearing the Emperor himself. He wore full uniform and the pith helmet in which he had so frequently been photographed.

The Lion of Judah embarked on the Boston Whaler and sat down amidships, surrounded by his bodyguards. Emil was forward in the prow. It was a full complement. But the Emperor's chief personal bodyguard was still on the shore. Despite all our protestations he insisted that he too must come aboard. He must have weighed about eighteen stone. The only place for him was the back near the engine in the stern of the boat, which was why we were protesting. With this extra load the boat was likely to capsize and the engine fail to function. The giant bodyguard refused to budge. Somehow the boat cast off and moved out on to the lake.

Suddenly a Mercedes drew up at the lake shore. More bodyguards piled out of it, carrying inflatable rubber rafts. As they blew them up we saw to our amazement that the rafts were circular. The would-be rowers stripped off their uniforms, revealing beneath only singlets and brief trunks, with machine pistols slung over their shoulders. They pushed their rafts out on to the lake and began to row: but they simply turned in circles. By this time the Boston Whaler was approaching the pelican colony. Amidships the main bodyguards were frantically bailing.

Emil shouted, 'For God's sake trans-ship that mountain of a man!' At last the bodyguard yielded. With some difficulty he was transferred to my small boat, which nearly turned over. When we returned to our embarkation point, the rafts were rotating. They had progressed little more than a hundred yards from the shore.

Next a motorcade was formed, with the Emperor at the head, and we drove to Lake Shala. At intervals Galla tribesmen lined the route. On

each occasion the Emperor stopped and handed out gifts. Later we discovered that he was giving them buns. At Shala Emil had arranged a picnic with little tents, umbrella-shaded tables, refreshments of all kinds. The Emperor relaxed.

He had clearly enjoyed himself. The Rift Valley National Park had existed nominally for several years, but the authorities concerned had shown little interest in it. Now the Emperor threw his weight into the scales. On the spot, at Shala, he decreed that the park should be included in the official government gazette. That did the trick.

Soon after this I had another encounter with royalty. I was invited to attend the Royal Premiere of the film *Now or Never*, which was held at London's National Film Theatre. The Queen, the Duke of Edinburgh and other members of the British Royal Family were there. I am glad to say that the film was greeted with warm applause, and was subsequently praised in the press.

After the premiere we were all invited to a buffet dinner at St James's Palace. Everyone was talking about the film. Suddenly Aubrey Buxton

Disguised, I was able to get close to the birds
and photograph their every activity.

said to me, 'Come on, I want you to meet the Queen'. He led me through the crowd into an adjoining room with dinner table set and a huge buffet table on the side with chefs standing beside it, at which the Queen was helping herself to some food.

Aubrey introduced me and then made off, leaving me standing alone with the Queen. Unfortunately, just at this moment I broke out in profuse perspiration. It was quite extraordinary, something that has never happened to me before or since. I was rendered speechless.

The Queen, realizing something of my predicament, said 'I very much enjoyed your film'. This made me feel considerably easier.

So I said, 'Ma'am, I have to apologise but I am terribly nervous, much more than if I were being charged by a herd of elephants'. She laughed and told me there was no reason to be nervous.

I smiled back, feeling slightly more relaxed, and proceeded to fill my plate without really thinking what I was doing.

When I turned round Her Majesty glanced at my plate and said 'That looks interesting'. I looked at my plate and realized what she meant. I had put meats and desserts all on the same plate.

By now I was literally bathed in sweat. I turned to look for a seat and found the only one was next to the Queen. I hadn't the courage to go and sit down. But Aubrey Buxton came up and said, 'You're supposed to sit next to the Queen'. So there was nothing for it.

Fortunately Her Majesty did not refer to my plate again, which eased my discomfort somewhat; and from then on we had a marvellous conversation about Africa. The Queen told me stories about her own favourite experiences there, and about the time her mother had been chased up a tree by a rhinoceros.

7 The Desert of the Danakil

Steaming sulphur springs, volcanoes active and extinct, great black rocks so hot they blistered your hand when you touched them, the temperature rising to 148°F and more, flat expanses of desert where the sand was so hot it blistered your feet even through thick shoes, and a Muslim people hardened by one of the most inhospitable environments in the world: that was the Danakil desert.

Sultan Ali Mirah Hanfare, ruler of these warrior tribes and their desolate land, lived in Asaita, on the edge of the desert. I got my first glimpse of the world of the Danakil when I visited Asaita with Colin and Joan Willock, and we were granted an audience with the Sultan.

Colin and I told Joan when we arrived at his palace that it was the invariable rule in this primitive Muslim country that a woman should walk behind her man. We were confounded therefore when she was ushered into the Sultan's presence ahead of us.

The Danakil tribesmen are hawk-nosed, slim and lean. By contrast their Sultan was an individual of vast proportions. But this was as it should be: he was their overlord. He showed us great courtesy. When we left Joan asked the Sultan, through an interpreter, whether she might photograph him. He agreed; and her picture was the only still taken of this impressive man. Although I filmed him I never managed to get a good still photograph.

The next day I saw the Sultan's second-in-command in action. He was known as Fetaurari. The occasion of our meeting was a strike of labourers in the nearby cotton plantation. An unruly crowd had gathered outside the plantation gates, and was trying to break in.

Fetaurari was quite an old man, but lean and fit. He was clad in a white shirt with a red sash round his waist. On his feet were rough Danakil sandals. His hair was white and he wore a Muslim cap. But it was his eyes that I shall never forget. They were piercing, like those of the eagle; they looked right through you.

I was in the plantation office when Fetaurari came in. He was accompanied by two bodyguards, dressed in the traditional robes, but with the modern addition of two army 303 rifles and a belt of ammunition. On his waist was a Buntline Special. The manager of the plantation, despite the support of twenty-five armed policemen flown in from Addis, had totally failed to control the threatening mob. Fetaurari said to him, 'You do not know how to deal with these people. Let me show you.' Then, followed by his two bodyguards, he advanced slowly towards the plantation gate.

As they saw him approach the crowd grew quieter. He told the gatekeepers to open the gate. Everybody was stunned into silence. He demanded to see the leader of the strikers – with whom the plantation officials had vainly been trying to negotiate. The leader came forward and stood in front of him. There was a moment of suspense, then suddenly Fetaurari spat in the man's face and smacked him resoundingly on each cheek. He followed this by telling the crowd that if everyone had not dispersed in one minute those left would be shot. One minute later they had all gone.

When I saw him again I asked Fetaurari if I might take his photograph. Willingly, he replied, but not now, later. Alas, there was no 'later'. I had to leave at once for Addis Ababa. When I next returned to Ethiopia Fetaurari was dead.

The Forbidden Desert of the Danakil (1973) was my second Ethiopian film. I decided to begin by taking aerial films of the landscape, covering the whole of this wild desert east of Addis Ababa. I hired a helicopter from Ethiopian Airlines and was lucky enough to secure the skilled airman Guy Dervieux as my pilot. He was fully aware of the difficulties that a helicopter would meet with in this area. I was to be enormously thankful for his presence.

The vibration of a helicopter, so different from that of an aeroplane, makes steady photography from the air extremely difficult. I decided that I would have to bolt my camera securely to the frame of the machine, and this called for a new mount, which I could construct myself. Mount and flying cost I calculated at about £1,500. I phoned Anglia and Aubrey Buxton agreed to this expense. It was risky; what if my mount proved to be a failure?

Addis Ababa is so high above sea level that aircraft cannot fly heavily

The Danakil tribesmen are hawk-nosed,
slim and lean.

loaded. On our first attempt at take-off the helicopter hovered; but when Guy pushed the stick forward to gain speed the skids immediately hit the tarmac again. For several minutes we went leap-frogging round the aerodrome; but it was no good, our equipment was too heavy. I chartered a Cessna 185 to bring our offload to Dessie, where the desert proper begins.

Between us and Dessie lay a range of ridged mountains rising to twelve thousand feet, well beyond the helicopter's capacity. The only hope was a thermal, a column of hot rising air similar to the one the pelicans use at Lake Shala. We flew along the side of one of the lower ridges and found one: then luckily at about ten thousand feet we found a saddle in the mountain chain and cleared it by twenty-five feet.

In front of us was a lonely, desolate landscape, with only a few tiny fields on which we might land in an emergency. The emergency soon happened. The helicopter started to shudder, and the engine kept missing. We saw a flat pinnacle of rock ahead and Guy decided to make a forced landing.

When we got out and checked we found that the mechanics who had serviced the plane at Addis Ababa had left water in the gasoline tank. They had endangered our lives by this carelessness. We drained the water, refilled the tank and gave it another try. Guy put the machine into a hover above the tiny piece of ground for a few minutes and took off once more; but again we had to descend, this time on one of the tiny fields. Before we put down there was not a single human being in sight. Directly we landed the whole landscape came alive with Ethiopian highlanders converging on us from every direction. They were too amazed to be hostile. They thronged round the helicopter chattering loudly. We made another attempt to drain the water, and re-started the engine. Only then did the highlanders disperse in alarm, leaving a space free for take-off. Soon we reached the escarpment and headed down into the Danakil desert.

We flew on over vast expanses of desert flats studded with dry, drab black rocks. It might have been a moonscape. At last we reached Tendaho, on the edge of the desert, and here we spent the night.

The next morning we took aerial shots of the Sultan's capital, Asaita, then followed the course of the mysterious Awash river between lakes and extinct volcanoes to the great evaporation pan known as Lake Abbe, where the river mysteriously disappears.[1] As we hovered over the lakeshore huge crocodiles bestirred themselves irritably. With lashing tails they moved off at surprising speed. As we flew low above the water

[1] See Wilfred Thesiger's *Arabian Sands* for a full description.

about thirty thousand flamingoes rose from the lake. It was one of the most beautiful sights I have seen in Africa. The sky was a wash of colour – softest pink shading into white and then nothing as they rose into what seemed empyrean heights, out of our vision. We approached one of the extinct volcanoes and found that, extinct though it might be, its crater was still hot enough to cause thermal updraughts which made the helicopter shudder violently.

Our next expedition from Tendaho was to Makalle in the north-west of the Danakil lands, to visit the governor of the region. On the way we passed over a fantastic landscape, a wild, rugged terrain beyond imagining. Huge cracks appeared in the ground, with steam pouring out of them. Where the highlands began the altitude of the land rose abruptly from two hundred to ten thousand feet. A violent heat haze covered the ground so that often we could not see it. In a tiny crater in which a waterhole had formed we saw a single Danakil hut.

Yet man has lived and worked in this desolate, frightening country for thousands of years. We landed near a crater, discovered first by Guy and Professor Haroun Tazieff, where Guy showed me an ancient work site, with fragments of weapons of all shapes and sizes; axes, spearheads, long knives – forerunners of those with which the Danakil tribes still slaughter and maim each other and any foreigners who trespass on their lands. It is clear from the remains that the fashioners of these weapons worked only in a mineral called obsidian.

At Makalle the governor, Ras Mengesha Seyoum, a relation of the Emperor, gave us permission to visit the Dallol depression. The next day we took off very early and flew east. At Dallol we had to meet an escort of the Ras's men for our protection.

The Dallol depression is the end of the earth, or maybe its beginning. It is 370 feet below sea level. Millions of years ago, geologists tell us, it was part of the Red Sea. It is the site of old salt, phosphate and sulphur workings, and bizarre rock formations. As we flew over it we saw a land of sulphur springs, of sulphur bubbling yellow, then turning brown, of sulphur steam pouring from fissures in the rock, of the nauseating smell of sulphur which penetrated every cranny of the helicopter.

Nearby we saw the salt lake of Karum, a flat crust concealing three thousand feet of solid salt. The native salt miners live in huts made of salt. A few years ago some Europeans attempted to mine this salt, but they had to give up because the climate was too much for them. On the day we visited it the ground temperature was 129.2°F. That day we flew over an active volcano. Fortunately Guy had been warned by Professor Tazieff of the sudden downdraughts we might encounter; and so I had the rare experience of filming an active volcano.

In three days I had photographed a great deal of scenery. But scenery without Danakil people would not make a film, and from all accounts photographing the people would be well-nigh impossible. Everyone I had spoken to had told me that the Danakil hated being photographed, and might kill a would-be photographer. Two Germans and an Italian exploring the desert recently had met exactly that fate. Their mutilated bodies told a grisly story. For a few days I had a fit of deep depression, and was ready to give up altogether.

But fortunately I did not. I decided to go back to Tendaho and look for a Danakil who could speak English. I was lucky, and found him in the shape of Ismail Mohamed Ismail, who incidentally was a friend of the Sultan's son Han Feri, no small recommendation. He took me to Asaita where we were joined by three armed bodyguards. The Danakil who came into Asaita were allowed to carry only sticks and knives, although the latter looked ominous enough.

It was Tuesday, the traditional market day in the town, when Danakil tribesmen from all over the desert bring in their wares and produce for barter or sale. I hoped this might be an opportunity to get my photographs, and I installed my camera on the first floor of a building overlooking the market place. It had a 500-millimetre telescopic lens.

But then I had a problem. I wanted to photograph the Danakil tribesmen and their wives, but mingling in the market place with them were scores of Ethiopian highlanders who were working in the Sultan's cotton plantations. Emphatically this was not the picture I wanted. I wanted just Danakil.

I had seen in the main street a bar-cum-liquor shop, especially established for the workers from the highland plateau. I went in, and to the astonishment of the proprietor asked if I could buy his entire stock of beer which amounted to about one hundred and fifty bottles. He hesitated, staring at me in disbelief, but I showed him my money, the deal was completed and I asked Ismail to spread the news around the market place that in ten minutes' time free beer would be available in this shop. Now to the Muslim Danakil all strong drink, even watered beer, was strictly forbidden, but the Christian highlanders suffered from no such inhibitions. In no time the market place was cleared of highlanders, and my coast was clear. Now I could get all the scenes I had envisaged; I was very excited.

I was captivated by the beauty of the young Danakil women. Their

The young Danakil women were strikingly beautiful and totally unself-conscious.

features were finely drawn, their bodies erect and magnificent. Young married women wore transparent black veils of fine gauze over their heads and breasts. The unmarried girls were bare-chested, and they were totally unself-conscious. The Danakil men would have taken violent exception to their women being photographed, so it was essential for me to remain hidden in order to film them.

The next day Ismail and I went to a hot spring geyser deep in the desert. It consisted of two huge basins of bubbling, boiling water. Some Danakil had followed us, and they were distinctly hostile. I knew that I would be courting disaster if I even attempted to film them, so instead I got out my camera and let them see it. Ismail explained to them that it was a magic box. To a Danakil it would be bad luck to touch such an object.

On the spur of the moment I beckoned to one of the Danakil, inviting him to inspect the camera. He approached hesitantly, and looked through the lens at one of his fellows. Then, by accident, I pressed the shutter release button. There was a sharp click as the shutter moved. A Danakil had photographed another Danakil.

There was a roar of rage, and the victim of photography pointed his rifle at me. I gathered from their gestures that his companions were demanding that I be thrown into the boiling basin. I was standing with my back to it, only ten feet away. Ismail intervened. The foreigner was the friend of Han Feri, the Sultan's son: he was befriended by the Sultan himself. The Danakil hesitated, talking among themselves.

By then I had managed to retreat to the car. A Danakil cried out, 'Very well then, let the foreigner throw the magic box down the basin.' This was the last thing I wanted to do: the camera was a Rolleiflex that had cost me more than £500. Protected temporarily by the fact that no Danakil would dare to touch the 'magic box' I turned round and quietly took the camera out of its case. Then, with every appearance of reluctance, I threw the case, and the case only, into the boiling cauldron. Judging by their faces the warriors seemed satisfied, but it might so easily have been me that was dissolved in brine. Ismail and I got into the car and drove carefully away. He told me quietly that it had been a very close call indeed.

A year later I paid my last visit to the Danakil, with Lee. This time

Steaming sulphur springs, blistering volcanic rocks and burning sand: the Danakil desert is one of the most inhospitable places in the world.

when I reached Asaita Ismail introduced me to his friend Ibrahim, who was much respected among the Danakil. There were two things in particular I wanted to see and film – the traditional Danakil game of *kosso*, and the Danakil war dance.

The first was not difficult to arrange: *kosso* is played with a tiny leather ball – a mixture of American football and English rugby, though much fiercer, often ending with knives flashing and the Sultan's bodyguard dragging the teams apart. I filmed the game in slow motion, low angle shots against the light. It turned out very well and when the Danakil film was shown I felt this was its highlight.

To arrange a war dance, Ibrahim explained, would be much more difficult. A bait was needed. I must buy ten cases of soft drinks and he would spread it abroad that they were being offered free for all. The result was miraculous. From the surrounding desert Danakil poured to

The Danakil's favourite sport is the game of kosso,
a kind of rugby played with a small leather ball.

the meeting place near the river, all of them armed to the teeth. They performed magnificently, with savage abandon.

The next day Ibrahim took me to visit an old man who worked as a blacksmith. He made knives and swords – though castration was now forbidden by law the Danakil paid little attention – out of car springs and other scraps of metal left behind by the Italians when they fled from Ethiopia in 1942. His bellows were made of goatskin.

On the way Ibrahim told me how expert the Danakil were at smuggling. If you ordered something from, say, a Japanese or Indian catalogue they would deliver it to you in six to twelve weeks by camel. This illicit trade had assumed such proportions, he added, that some cigarette makers now made boxes specially adapted for carrying on camels.

Lee and I, with Ibrahim and Ismail, drove out deep into the desert, where we found a herd of camels. (The Sultan owned nine thousand.)

*Possession of a waterhole is the
Danakil's chief guarantee of survival.
They will fight to the death for it.*

The herder was clearly a man of consequence. He asked how many camels we wanted for Lee. Laughingly I answered, 'About a thousand'. He took me perfectly seriously. When should he deliver them? I had to explain that she was not really for sale. I could not do without her, and I would not know what to do with the camels.

Later in the day we came upon a group of herders. They were intrigued by Lee's apparel, which consisted only of a shirt and blue jeans. Was she a man or a woman? They touched her, even felt her breasts, before they were satisfied. We were allowed to photograph the nomads, but in turn we had to submit to drinking their camels' milk. This is kept in a closely woven basket which has been dipped in camels' urine to

Right: A camel carries everything needed for the nomadic life.

Lee and I were welcomed with camel's milk, served in a woven basket that had been dipped in camels' urine to shrink it tight.

shrink it tight. The basket was passed all round. I knew they were doing us a great honour, so when my lips touched the black crust on the mouth of the basket I forced myself to swallow. The basket went round and round until we were nearly sick; but I got the film.

On our final expedition into the Danakil desert we visited a waterhole called Loma, many miles from Asaita, situated at the bottom of an extinct volcanic crater whose steep hillsides are strewn with black rocks. Lee and I were accompanied by Ibrahim and Ismail and an escort of two Danakil. We reached our destination in the early morning.

Possession of a waterhole is to the Danakil the chief guarantee of survival. They will fight to the death for it. There is a legend among them of a warrior killing thirteen attackers to defend his waterhole. Such battles still occur frequently, for in this desert life has changed little over centuries. Water means life; lack of it means almost certain death.

We sat on the crater's rim and viewed the lifeless bottom below. A wind came up and brought gusts of dust and tiny bits of rock flying against the cameras, some of which we had packed into plastic bags. Suddenly on the other side we saw two Danakil men and three children making their way over black lava rock into the crater. When they reached the bottom the crater carried their voices up to our ears like a giant sound reflector. The children, laughing happily, ran straight for a small hole in the ground, as children in other parts of the world run to a Coca-Cola stand.

The elder of the Danakil men climbed into this hole, filled up his goatbag and lifted it for the children to drink. Then they washed themselves, their dark bodies glistening in the sun. The men led the youngsters into the shade of a tiny bush and ordered them to wait, then the two men crossed the bottom of the crater, which was about a hundred yards in diameter, and made their way up towards us.

When they were halfway up Lee and one of our Danakil went into the crater to photograph some wild birds, which had arrived to drink. The men halted and looked suspicious, but not unduly worried. As Lee went on down the mountain the Danakil came towards us with stern faces. I felt they might be offended by our intruding into their territory, but as they approached they gave us a friendly 'Salam Aleikum'. Relieved, I answered 'Aleikum Salam'. Ismail proceeded to talk to them in their own tongue and explained that the *ferengis* meant no harm and were here merely to make a film.

A newborn lamb promises food,
drink and clothing.

After he had told them that we had the permission of the Sultan they seemed quite happy. The wind came on quite strongly now. We sat on the ridge while the air heated up. I gazed over the drab flatness of the desert, dotted with the odd hardy bush. Dust devils danced like fairies in the far distance. Then suddenly Ismail pointed to the east and some slowly moving dots emerged on the shimmering horizon. It was a group of nomads and camels making their way to the water.

I had my tripod set up, preparing to use the 200 millimetre lens. The nomads were still only specks in the endless desert. The burning dryness was accentuated by the powdery dust trailing behind them. An Egyptian vulture glided effortlessly overhead and descended slowly into the crater below, landing clumsily and searching for food.

Lee had got very close to the little desert birds and was clicking away happily. She seemed absolutely absorbed in her work, oblivious to the heat which crept up from the bottom of the crater. Rivulets of sweat appeared on her forehead and dripped into the hardened mud below.

The camel caravan was quite close now and we could see that there were five camels loaded with the modest possessions of the typical nomad, led by three women. Behind trailed two men, typically carrying rifles. With the 300 millimetre lens I could now make out every detail. They came closer and vanished behind a precipice which blocked the entrance to the crater from our view.

In the meantime, a woman with a baby on her back had appeared from nowhere and was heading straight for the waterhole where Lee was now photographing. Then two more men appeared. With all this activity Lee's birds vanished and she took her tripod and camera and retreated.

Just as Lee reached the rim of the volcano the women and camels came into view again. The camels were led gently down the steep embankment. The people seemed quite unconscious of our cameras. One of the men who had arrived earlier climbed into the waterhole, filled up his goatbag, and poured the water into a little natural trough where the camels took a long drink. It was striking to see that the nomads let their camels drink first, before they slaked their own thirst, indicating how much importance they attached to these peculiar animals. Without them they could not survive in the desert. The Danakil dig holes for water, feed meagre bits of grass and shrubs to their camels, and then live off the rich camel's milk.

The salt lake of Karum. Above: a camel caravan
waits to be loaded with salt blocks. Below:
native miners use sticks to dislodge the salt
from the lake's crust.

Suddenly the waterhole became a hive of activity. Herds of goats stormed down the sides to get to the water. I decided to go down into the crater in order to get close-ups of the people. Slowly Ismail, Ibrahim and I edged our way down the steep side. Some of the Danakil stopped digging, watching us with suspicion as we descended. The first one to come towards us was obviously a particularly respected man. Ismail and Ibrahim sounded a friendly 'Salam Aleikum'. The men, armed with a rifle, repeated 'Aleikum Salam'. Ismail explained that we were trying to make a film about the Danakil, which had never been done before, and that our visit was sanctioned by the Sultan. We gave him some cigarettes but when I slowly lifted my camera to film, his face changed, expressing deep suspicion. Disregarding this I pressed on, and by giving out more cigarettes and especially matches, we were finally accepted.

Lee and I were able to get some remarkable footage to complete our film on these primitive people and their strange wild world. Tragically, since we were there, the Danakil have been practically wiped out. Their Sultan was deposed in the Ethiopian revolution, and the people massacred by government forces. Like many of the animals we have filmed in Africa, the Danakil have fallen victim to modern man's cruelty and greed.

Young married women wore transparent black veils over their heads and breasts: the unmarried girls went barebreasted.

PART FOUR *Tanzania and Kenya*

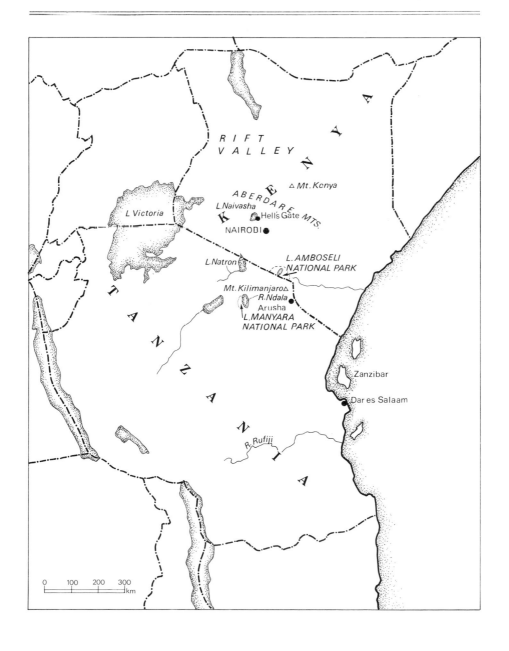

Lake Manyara National Park is over-populated with elephants, who are in danger of ruining their own environment.
Right: young bulls play-fighting.

8 Trumpets and Balloons

I was privileged to meet in Africa a number of people who had the gift of establishing an instant rapport with wild animals. Two of them were Iain and Oria Douglas-Hamilton, whose book *Among the Elephants* is regarded as a classic. Two others were Alan and Joan Root, who apart from their gift with animals are also obsessed with balloons.

On one occasion when I was in London Colin Willock summoned me to ask my help. A young British scientist, Iain Douglas-Hamilton, and his wife Oria had been living for several years at Lake Manyara National Park in Tanzania. Iain had just finished writing a thesis on elephants. They had also shot a great deal of film, which Anglia had agreed to buy. It included one astonishing scene of a large elephant cow smashing up Iain's Land-Rover and driving her tusks through the cabin in which Iain was sitting; and another in which several females tried to lift up a darted young elephant – truly sensational stuff. But there was not enough to make a one-hour *Survival* special. Would I help Douglas-Hamilton to finish it off?

At first I was reluctant. Hitherto all my films for Anglia had been started and finished by me. However, when I met Iain and his wife I took an instant liking to them, and I agreed.

Lake Manyara National Park lies in the Rift Valley of Tanzania. It ·extends thirty miles along the shores of Lake Manyara, which is never more than five miles wide, with the high hills of the Rift often descending sheer to its shore. Compared with Etosha or Serengeti it is a very small park, but it is a place of immense natural beauty. However it is overpopulated by elephants, who are destroying the *acacia tortilis* trees, and unless they are controlled and protected the elephants will destroy themselves by ruining the environment in which they live. This was the reason for Iain's study.

Lee and I flew to Nairobi, chartered a plane to Manyara, and took a car to join Iain. When we reached the main road leading to Arusha our

Tanzanian driver suddenly applied the brakes. Coming towards us at high speed, though with plenty of room to stop, was a beige Peugeot station wagon with a red light flashing. It mounted the verge, missing us by perhaps a foot, and was gone. Just as my driver managed to stop I saw another car, this time a red-brown Mercedes, approaching at equal speed. We could just see two men sitting on the back seat, before the car was upon us. We were helpless: surely this time it could not avoid us. By some miracle it did, and vanished in a cloud of dust. My driver threw up his hands in horror.

'Do you know who that was?' asked the driver. 'President Mobuto and President Nyerere!'

We found Iain and Oria at the Warden's home. Iain immediately took me out on tour. On the first day we were accompanied by the park's Chief Warden, Benjamin Kanza, and spent the night at Iain's old camp on the N'dala river. The next day, as we drove through the park, we sighted three elephants ahead, one of them under a tree.

'You may get a good charge,' Iain said, keeping the car going. No sooner said than done. The elephant came at us like a steamroller, to within six feet. Iain drove just fast enough through the bush to stay in front of the charging cow. With my wide-angle camera, which I managed to hold, arms outstretched, pointed at the elephant, I got some excellent shots, while the elephant screamed violently. Then she shook her head, trumpeted and turned back, just as my film ran out. She had followed us for ninety seconds.

Another time Iain pointed to an elephant, remarked, 'That's a nice cow,' and stopped the car. Something in his manner made me suspect that he was playing games. He was. Without warning the 'nice' cow charged right up to the car, trumpeting loudly. I flinched, just as Iain had hoped.

'I believe,' he said, 'that's the first time anyone has seen you flinch.' It was a hoax elephant; it was in fact his favourite, Boadicea, the leader of a family unit with which he was on the closest terms. (The leader of an elephant family group is always the senior female.)

Other elephants were more docile. One day we stopped close to a group of elephants. One of the cows was standing with her back to us. Iain called gently, 'Virgo, Virgo'. Immediately the cow turned round, came straight to the car, followed by her calf, and put her trunk in Iain's hand. He had not seen her for two years.

Overleaf: a school of hippos crosses the narrow Rift Valley lake.

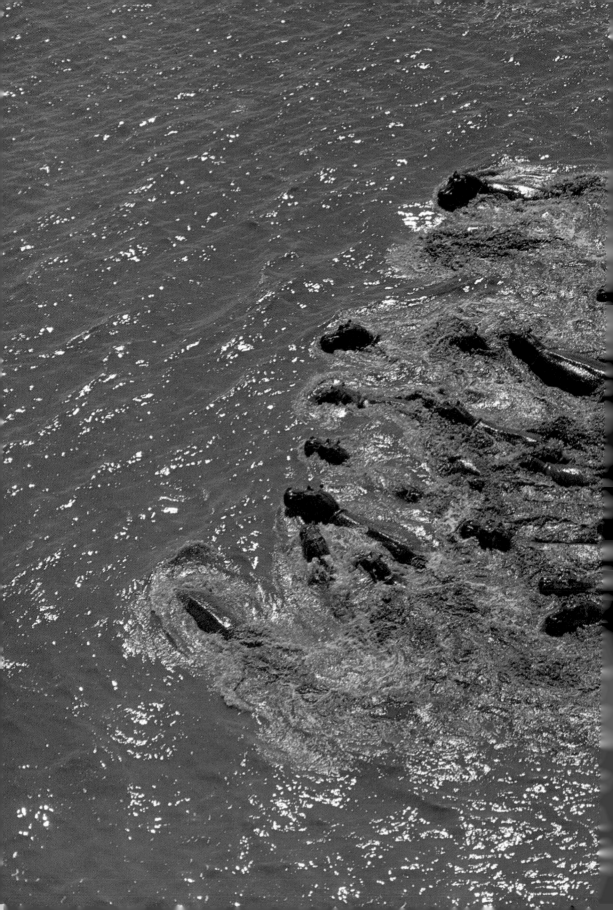

There was a buffalo to scare me too. He started charging unexpectedly while we were driving along the beach. Iain swerved and turned the car around, and the old buffalo followed. I sat fully exposed in the back of the car with my camera. At the last moment he swerved, only a couple of yards away, and galloped down the beach and into the lake. Fortunately I got an excellent shot of him.

Arriving late one night after dark we found all the bedclothes of Iain's tent lying about outside in the sand. In the light of Iain's torch we could make out lion pugmarks in the sand. They had obviously used Iain and Oria's bed as a romping ground. They had chewed blankets, which were still covered with their saliva. Sand was flung everywhere and the zip of the tent had been broken. The lions had only just left: perhaps our approach had hastened their departure. Later that night we were woken up by a loud noise. Lions again? No, it was simply a big branch falling from a tree right on to Iain's tent.

We were visited at Lake Manyara by Colin Willock, the *Survival* writer, and Alan Root. Alan Root is a fine naturalist cameraman, a keen conservationist and a highly skilled and daredevil flier. His film *The Year of the Wildebeest* is, to my mind, the greatest wildlife film ever made. He had joined us now to help film some aerial shots. Later he and Iain went together to a conservation conference at the Serengeti Research Institute. Their departure was spectacular. I watched as they took off and their plane disappeared over the escarpment. Lee and I were in our car on the road. Suddenly we heard a roar and almost simultaneously a bang as the plane's wheels skimmed the car roof. Root continued his dive until the main wheels of his Cessna were nearly touching the road, then he pulled out of it, banked steeply and vanished into the distance.

It was in conjunction with this remarkable airman that I carried out one of my most rewarding assignments on the African continent. Alan and Joan Root were balloon freaks. They were determined to fly in a hot-air balloon on a route no one had ever attempted before, including flying right over the summit of Mount Kilimanjaro, the highest peak in Africa.

It seemed a hopeless project. A hot-air balloon has a minimum of self-control and a marked reluctance to yield to control by others. It is at the mercy of every wind that blows, of every updraught and down-draught of air. Neither it nor its pilot can prevent it dashing itself against any escarpment that looms ahead, or descending into thick jungle or a volcano's crater.

How could their balloon, albeit the very latest model of its kind, equipped with a powerful extra flame-booster which when used made a

Iain Douglas-Hamilton knows his elephants backwards.

noise like a clap of thunder, be coaxed over the top of a mountain more than eighteen thousand feet high? The short answer was that by the time I arrived on the scene the Roots had achieved the impossible – and had also taken two hundred feet of film.

Enter Anglia Television. Colin Willock was quick to see the chance. Expand what the Roots had photographed into a hour-long film covering every aspect of what this balloon could be made to do, call it *Balloon Safari* ('Safari' is always an evocative word) and get Dieter Plage and Bob Campbell to help Alan film it. That was how it came about that I found myself a guest of the Roots – and their numerous wildlife pets – at their home on the shores of Lake Naivasha, awaiting the arrival of an identical second balloon.

The second balloon was necessary to get the maximum coverage: the occupants of each dressed identically to preserve illusion – could photograph one another. On our first flight the two balloons were to take off in sequence and the four of us were to take photographs of each other as we

The brightly coloured envelopes, filled with hot air,
sailed high over the herds of wildebeeste.

dodged in and out of the clouds which that morning covered most of
Lake Naivasha. The balloons were spread out on the lake shore and into
them in the cool morning air the burner thundered an eight-foot flame.
Slowly the brightly coloured envelopes filled with hot air until they
stood erect, ready for lift-off.

Phil Dunnington, Alan's balloon instructor, flew the second balloon,
with me as his passenger. We took off first and below us we could see
Alan and Joan slowly gliding over the lake's papyrus thickets. We started
rising rapidly and suddenly we were in cloud so thick that although Phil
was only four feet away from me I could scarcely see him. The burner
thundered again, the cloud began to thin out and suddenly we were
floating in the heavens. Through a gap below us we could see the lake
and through another gap Alan's balloon. The cloud seemed to glow pink
and then orange as the other balloon forced its way through to the top.

Now both balloons were 'in the clear'. Alan decided to ascend higher,
then descended rapidly so that I could film him plunging into cloud. He
disappeared completely, and the next thing we heard of him was on the

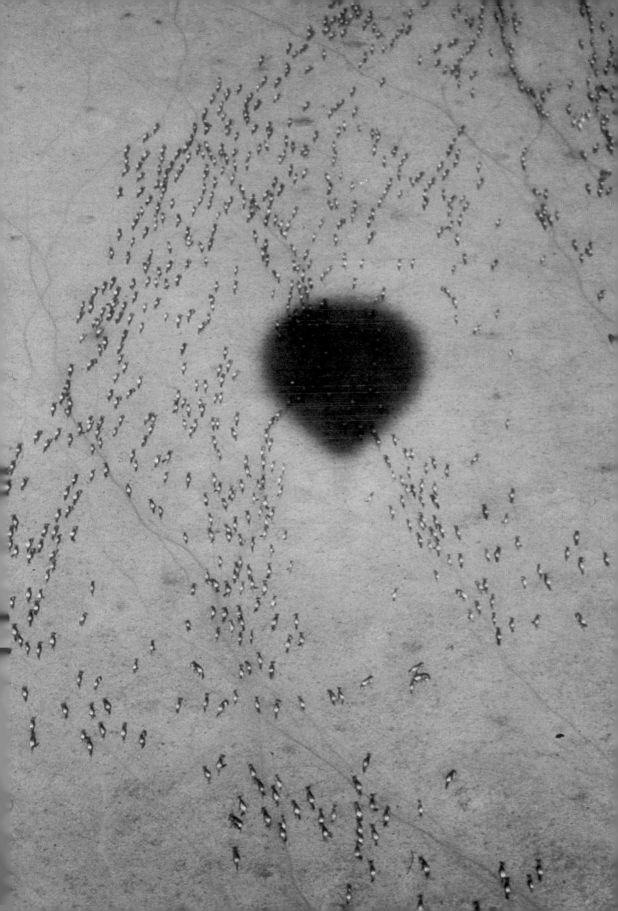

radio, telling us that he had managed to catch a wind which had taken him towards Hell's Gate, and advising us to descend, as the cloud base was now much lower; he himself had just managed to find a landing place.

It was up to Phil, with whatever assistance his inexperienced companion could give him, to do likewise. By now we could see only a few faint glimpses of the lake, so Phil decided to climb higher. Lacking a compass we had no idea in which direction we were going, so in order to orientate himself Phil lined up the top of Mount Kenya, visible in the distance, with the top of the nearer Aberdare mountains. We climbed higher, higher, till we reached approximately eighteen thousand feet, and a wind to head back towards Hell's Gate. When Phil estimated we had gone far enough east he stopped 'burning' and we began to descend. He held his hand outside the balloon's basket as the only possible way of checking our rate of descent: the wind rushing through your fingers gives an indication of your speed.

Minutes went by; we transferred the burner pipe to the last gas cylinder, and then we heard Alan's voice on the radio again warning us to descend as slowly as possible as the cloud base was only a few hundred feet above a mountain ridge. The burner was still in action, checking our rate of descent. It got darker and darker. Suddenly a westerly wind sprang up and we were out of the cloud, descending far too quickly towards the ridge of an extinct volcano. It seemed as if we must hit it. Relentlessly the wind drifted us towards a likely sudden death.

We cleared the ridge by two feet.

The next obstacle on our downward way was a steep rock face. We knew we were not going to make this one, and sure enough we hit the mountainside. With part of its weight now supported by the cliff wall the balloon gathered momentum, and we were pulled more and more rapidly and scrapingly upwards. To make matters worse, the basket caught behind a rock and the balloon's pulling power caused it, in balloon parlance, to dogbox (i.e. to turn upside-down). We clung on for dear life with a sheer hundred-foot drop beneath us.

Although Phil at once stopped burning when the balloon reached the top of the cliff, we had already injected so much heat in order to get the balloon free that we shot violently skywards before Phil could open the airflaps to reduce lift. We were now however very low on fuel, and an

In order to orientate ourselves we lined up the top of Mount Kenya, in the distance, with the peaks of the Aberdare Mountains.

*After landing, a gust of wind caught the balloon
and dragged it violently along the ground.*

immediate landing was essential. I could see only one small landing
space, covered with scrub, hardly an inviting prospect. Phil told me
what he proposed to do.

'When I've descended to about sixty feet I'm going to pull the ripcord.
This will mean that the top of the balloon will be pulled away. The air
will escape in a massive burst, we shall descend at great speed and we
shall have a very hard landing.' I readied myself while Phil put his plan
into operation and the balloon fell rapidly towards the ground. I waited
nervously for the jolting impact. To my astonishment all that happened
was a gentle thud. The balloon bounced unalarmingly and then fell on its
side, the red-orange envelope settling quietly into the bushes. It was a
picture-book landing performed by a master balloonist. We were completely out of fuel.

Shortly after our narrow escape on the mountain ridge we had an
encounter with the Masai. They are a pastoral people, and the fiercest of
all the Kenya tribes. One day while filming we force-landed in a volcanic
area and had to enlist the help of a group of Masai to carry the balloon out
to where we had left the carrier vehicle. A bargain was struck – they
would help only if afterwards we would take them for a balloon ride. We

agreed, and next day at the appointed time we fetched them in the Land-Rover from their *manyatta* (homestead) near a large pan at Amboseli. Alan had the balloon stretched out on the ground. While he lit the flame they looked on in amazement, and when he turned on the burner the thunderous noise frightened even the sturdiest of the warriors, who scattered in all directions, returning only when Alan turned it off.

Finally the balloon was fully inflated. The Masai clambered into the basket laughing and pushing and, as the balloon took off, with me hanging on and trying to film, they cried excitedly *'Kwenda Juu!'* ('Higher, higher!'). But the most fantastic thing to them was not the fact that they were flying, but that they could see their beloved cattle from the air, moving across the plain in long rows with dust blowing lazily over the barren ground.

After we had made the flight we went back to the volcanic area and spread the balloon out on the rock in order to film the Masai carrying it. After we had finished the warriors immediately lay down under a tree, using round balls of elephant dung as headrests, and went to sleep. The Masai sleep mostly during the hot part of the day. At night they stay awake, to guard their *manyatta* and cattle against marauding lions.

One day we landed in a Masai *manyatta* and were immediately surrounded by warriors holding spears and women wearing beautiful beadwork around their necks. Many of the warriors had Kodak film cans hanging from their ears: they used them for storing their tobacco. I began to film the Masai as they clustered round the balloon, but like a flash one old warrior rushed up to me and demanded payment. I told him I would not film any more, and turned my viewfinder away so that the Masai would think I was filming the surroundings. But I reversed my viewfinder, and thus I got some first-rate pictures, particularly of some of the *morans* (younger warriors), one of whom told me that in the last three weeks he had killed three lions with a spear.

We went to Amboseli National Park in the hope of filming the balloon flying over a herd of elephants in front of Mount Kilimanjaro. This was one of the scenes which so far had eluded us. Despite a strong adverse wind we got the balloon into the air, with Alan and Joan aboard. Mike Price and I were in a Range-Rover. Presently Alan called me on the walkie-talkie to tell me that he had spotted a herd of elephants which might be suitable for filming. We hurried to the spot he had mentioned. The elephants were on the right, looking towards us. Slowly the balloon approached and moved past Kilimanjaro. Just at that moment the elephants moved to the left and we had all of them placed perfectly in the picture. This was one of the most memorable moments of the film: it was the sequence we had been waiting for.

Several weeks later we were ready to return to Naivasha. The balloon recovery crew set off in the forward control Land-Rover, I followed in a second Land-Rover full of equipment, and the two remaining members of the team, Mike Moore, the second ballonist, and 'Big Tuna' Harris (so-called because of the outrageous stories he used to tell about the Chicago gangster Big Tuna Accardo) drove a Range-Rover with a trailer. As we made our way down a steeply descending winding road, one of the wheels of the trailer suddenly fell off. While the rest of us were trying to work out a way of loading the trailer on top of another vehicle, Mike Moore and Big Tuna stopped a group of Masai and made a deal with them. If they would help us hoist the trailer on to the forward control Land-Rover we would give them a lift back to their *manyatta*. Somehow we got the trailer hoisted into position, somehow we bundled the Masai into our vehicles. It was a very tight squeeze and soon the smell of buttric acid combined with sweat became almost unbearable. Every so often Mike and Big Tuna would stick their heads out of the window; they were coming up for air!

We drove thus for about an hour, until the passengers in the Range-Rover indicated that they wanted to get out. One of them was hunched up and holding his crotch. The other Masai asked him what was wrong and the hunched one declared, according to Big Tuna, that he would never again travel in that particular sort of vehicle as it had frozen his testicles. The Range-Rover had been so over-crowded that he had been pushed off his seat and had his crotch exposed to the full force of the car's air conditioning.

The last stage of our journey was marked by the complete brake failure of the balloon crew's Land-Rover. They came charging past us at about eighty-five miles an hour with both doors wide open to act as dive brakes. But the road flattened out before disaster occurred, a change down into third gear slowed the vehicle up and the whole expedition finally reached Naivasha in safety.

Giraffe and calf.

PART FIVE *Zaire*

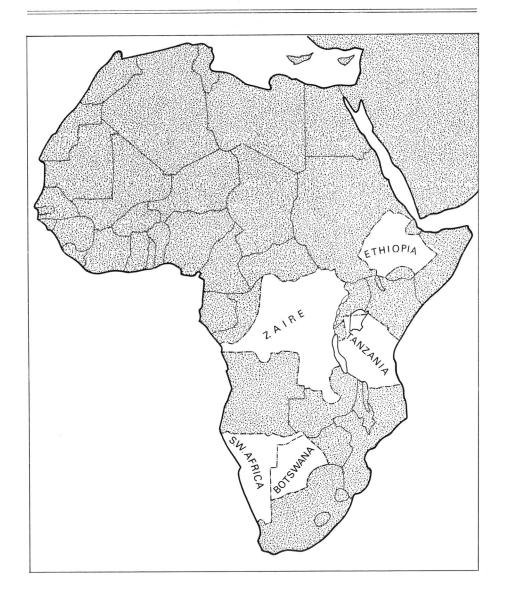

9 The Lords of the Forest

'*Kom, Kom, Kasimir; Kasimir Kom, Kom!*' There was an upheaval in the dense jungle, the leaves parted and there stood a magnificent specimen of the dwindling race of mountain gorillas. He paused for a moment, then charged.

The caller stood firm, and I, standing fifteen feet behind with my camera, managed to do the same, though my hands and knees were shaking. Kasimir, a huge silver-backed male, came face to face with his fellow primate, then halted and after a moment turned round and sat down about ten feet away.

The man who had called '*Kom, Kom, Kom*' is one of the most remarkable men I have ever known. His name is Adrien de Schryver.

Adrien is a Belgian who stayed behind when what was the Belgian Congo became independent. In the civil wars that followed he was sorely harassed, constantly in danger of being shot, his house was besieged and finally destroyed, his family evacuated across Lake Kivu to the neighbouring state of Rwanda. Yet he decided to remain.

The reason he stayed was the mountain gorillas: he lived in one of the few areas in the world where these magnificent apes still survived. He was determined that this sanctuary – the first real jungle, a dense rain forest, in which I had ever tried to photograph – should be preserved; and he knew that the only way to do this was to convert it into a national park.

In order to raise the necessary money he sent out appeals to wild life conservation bodies all over the world. The only reply came from Professor Grzimek of the Frankfurt Zoological Society, which provided

Adrien de Schryver was convinced that he could establish a rapport with the mountain gorillas: and because he was utterly without fear, he had succeeded.

Adrien with some funds when he most needed them. Later in 1970, President Mobutu of Zaire turned this mountainous rain forest area into the Kahuzi-Biega National Park.

I had first visited Adrien in May 1973. My journey was full of incident. On the last leg of the flight from Bujumbura, the capital of the independent state of Burundi, to Kinshasa, the capital of Zaire, the stewardess in the first-class section (there was no room in the economy class, so I had been promoted or 'upgraded' as they say in the airline business) handed round sachets of eau de Cologne tissues. Sitting in front of me was a high official of the Congo Republic. He looked at the sachet with a puzzled expression, opened it, took out the tissue, smelt it – and ate it.

Arrived in Kinshasa, I presented my passport to the official in charge, only to find that my visa had expired. The passport officer told me that I had two alternatives. I could spend the night in a Zaire gaol and be deported in the morning. This he would not recommend. Or I could have a comfortable sleep in a hotel, but this would not happen of course unless I showed my appreciation in the form of twenty Zaire (about twenty pounds sterling). Needless to say I paid. The taxi driver to the Inter-Continental Hotel also demanded twenty Zaire, but I won this battle. After a violent altercation I appealed to the hotel manager, who told me the correct fare was 7.50. I threatened to go straight to the police. The taxi driver accepted 7.50.

Kinshasa (formerly Leopoldville) has wide avenues, colourfully-dressed people, and the riverfront of the great Congo (now Zaire) river. It also has a market place, which sells everything from shoe-laces to enormous live grubs, wriggling in their baskets. I saw a lady approach the grub stall, pick up a grub and eat it. Obviously she found it delicious, for she promptly ordered another half-pound.

During my wanderings in Kinshasa I saw the base of a once-proud monument to King Leopold II of the Belgians which had been toppled by angry mobs during the civil war that followed Independence. More surprising was the unfinished monument of Zaire's first President, the murdered Patrice Lumumba. It consisted only of a giant finger pointing to the sky. My taxi-driver told me that the government had run out of money and could not finish it, but remembering the factions that had arisen during post-Independence days I wondered.

It took me six days to find, let alone clear, my baggage. This involved interviews with numbers of officials – not all of them well-disposed. I was not sorry to leave Kinshasa, nor did I relish the prospect of returning there a week later to meet Lee, who was to come and help me film Adrien de Schryver and his gorillas.

I finally arrived at Adrien's lovely lakeside home in Bukavu, armed

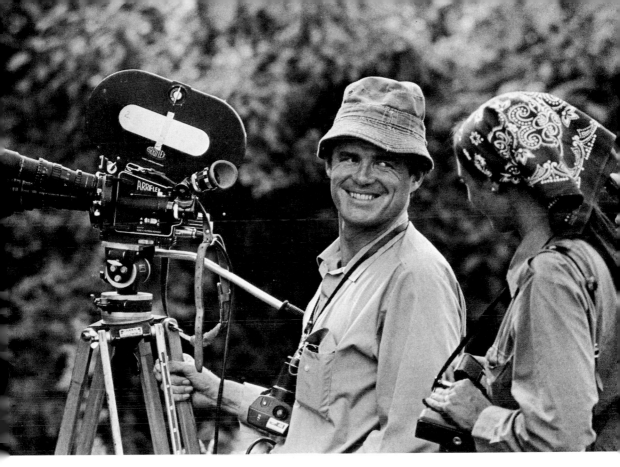

*Lee and I soon realised that there was
a marvellous film to be made about Adrien
and his gorillas.*

with an introduction from Professor Grzimek. I had decided that if after
six weeks of filming I had five minutes of usable footage, I would then,
with Adrien's agreement, stay on for six months to make an hour-long
film.

Adrien had been getting to know his gorillas for eight years. He had
studied their every movement at every season, their every habitat.
Kasimir, the grey-haired or 'silver-backed' patriarch, and his family of
eighteen males, females and young had come to accept his presence.
Adrien was convinced that, given time, he could establish a rapport with
these first cousins of man, and miraculously, and because he was utterly
without fear, he had succeeded. The image of the monster gorilla
embodied in films like *King Kong* should now be banished for ever.
Even the beating of the breast is known now to be an action to release
tension, rather than of aggression. So the call of '*Kom, Kom, Kasimir!*'
was often heard in the forest. Kasimir came, and Adrien went unharmed.

Kasimir, the leader of the group, was a magnificent silver-backed male. An adult gorilla eats at least sixty pounds of food every day.

On the occasion of my first view of Kasimir we foregathered at the gates of the national park with Adrien's two trackers, Patrice and Pili-Pili. The former was pure pygmy, dressed in army boots several sizes too large for him, a greatcoat and dark green beret. He carried a large and formidable *panga*, the heavy knife Africans use as both tool and weapon. He had the most infectious smile. Pili-Pili was bigger, only half-pygmy. Patrice shared Peter Stark's passion for honey, but more sensibly robbed the hives of stingless bees.

Patrice, who during my stay at Bukavu changed his name to Mushebere, was also very keen on *matabiche* (tips). When an American TV crew had come to Kahuzi-Biega he had used the large tip he was given to buy another wife. He also used tips to buy *pombe*, the native beer. When a friend of Adrien's brought his fourteen-year-old daughter to stay Mushebere took the father aside and asked him how much money or cattle he wanted for his daughter. The father politely pointed out that she was too young at fourteen to get married, and anyway was promised to another man. Mushebere said whatever the other man was offering, he would give him one more cow.

Mushebere had just come back from the forest and had located the gorillas. He spoke to Adrien in Swahili and waved his *panga*. We walked along the tar road cutting the park from east to west. Pili-Pili pointed into the jungle and we saw that some of the vegetation was trodden down. Clouds were moving in rapidly and the light was very poor. Everywhere the jungle was dense with the lush vegetation that thrived in the humid conditions: giant creepers hung down from the trees. Only Patrice with his *panga* could make a path. The odd droppings and remnants of a gorilla's meal were the only sign's. Adrien showed me a bitten-off plant. From the colour of the bitten part he could say how long ago the gorillas had come past. On we went, avoiding nettles, making our way slowly through the thick vegetation. I thought at first, 'How will we ever see anything in this dense forest?'; but then my heart began to race, some trees quite close by started moving and a short sharp call followed.

Adrien looked at us and demanded total silence. We were close to the Lords of the Forest. Then we saw a curious face eyeing us from the top of a tree and a hand gripping a giant creeper. Adrien calmly started plucking a few *bwamba* leaves, and ate them. He always did this when approaching the gorillas, as a sign that he came in peace. I was tense: I heard branches moving, and sharp barking calls. Adrien called: '*Kom, Kom, Kom, Kasimir!*' Kasimir let out a terrifying scream, and charged.

Adrien did not move. Man and gorilla eyed each other for a few seconds, and then Kasimir, resting on his enormous fore-arms, grumbled a bit, turned round, and sat down under a tree. Adrien stood there as if nothing had happened, chewing a few leaves. The trackers and I looked at each other and let out a sigh of relief.

One early African explorer wrote: 'Anyone letting a gorilla charge closer than eighty feet is a sheer madman'. Certainly Adrien had disproved this assertion. I shall never forget what I had just seen.

Although I was to face and film about thirty charges, some of them more determined and closer, this is the one I shall always remember because it was the first. While I was recovering from the shock the *bwamba* trees around us started moving and some females and infants climbed the branches to feed on the juicy leaves. It is estimated that an adult gorilla eats at least sixty pounds of food a day.

One male, whom we later called Hannibal, and who was the third in rank in the group, stood up on his back legs and drummed on his chest with his giant hands. Kasimir looked at us again and lay down under the tree for a lunchtime snooze. Slowly all the gorillas joined in the siesta. Next to eating, sleeping is their main activity.

We stood waiting in a little clearing Adrien had cut out. Suddenly the skies opened, and we were drenched with rain. Kasimir, who was lying under the tree, eyed us occasionally, as if to see how long we would stand it. When he had had enough he moved into deeper cover.

As soon as Lee joined me at Bukavu we went on another expedition into the forest with Adrien to find the gorillas. Kasimir seemed very edgy that day. The reason soon became clear: the fourth-ranking male gorillas, whom Adrien had named Fred, was pursuing one of Kasimir's wives. When the two lovers appeared together Kasimir veered off into the bush and punished the unfortunate youngster. The other gorillas meanwhile climbed a big tree full of juicy creepers. Adrien whispered, 'Get ready, Kasimir is going to climb'. Kasimir obliged, eating the creepers on his way up. More and more females followed him, until at one stage the tree bore a load of fourteen gorillas. So much for the widespread belief that the mountain gorilla does not climb trees.

After Kasimir had descended Musharamina, the Number Two, decided to stage a demonstration. First he charged us, but tentatively, staying behind bushes. The pygmies were terrified. He moved around us in circles, communicating occasionally with Kasimir, who was resting nearby in the shade of a huge *bwamba* tree. As we watched from our little clearing Musharamina made another quite determined charge.

Now Kasimir felt he had to show who was the boss, the dominant male. Adrien was standing looking into the thicket, I stood three feet to his left, slightly behind, and Lee behind both of us. Suddenly Kasimir burst through a curtain of creepers and made straight for Adrien, letting out the most terrifying screams. He stopped just short of Adrien and grabbed his shoe, still screaming as loud as he could, and showing two rows of yellowish fangs. Then he retreated and looked at us.

Adrien moved away to his left and calmly raised his camera to take Kasimir's picture. When the shutter clicked Kasimir charged again, but this time he came for me. My Arriflex 16 was running. I had the previous charge on film already, and I was determined to get this one. He came towards me screaming, and made straight for my feet. I did not move. I followed him with the camera until he was almost directly beneath it. Maybe it was the camera that deterred him from touching me. Then he veered off towards Adrien, retreated into the thicket and joined the family, which was now filing past.

Adrien looked back and saw Lee and me still there, shaking a bit, but still holding our cameras. He smiled and said, 'Congratulations, you made it'. Once before, apparently, he had taken a cameraman who, when Kasimir charged, had dropped his camera and run!

I think it was at this point that Adrien decided to let us carry on and make a film with him. And Lee and I realized that our film could be a fine tribute to this remarkable man.

One day Adrien, Lee and I decided to make an aerial reconnaissance flight. In marshy ground some way inside the Kahuzi-Biega Park we detected a hut with smoke coming from it. We decided to investigate. With us went Mushebere and four armed guards. As we approached the confines of the park we questioned several villagers. They seemed strangely apprehensive. When we found a well-trodden path leading into the park our suspicions were confirmed. We walked for two hours, then Mushebere pointed to recent human spoor. Soon we came upon two poachers, caught red-handed removing a rock-hyrax[1] from a trap. Adrien and the guards rushed them, hand-cuffed them and took them along with us.

Later our little band separated. The ground was growing marshier: we felt we were nearing the poachers' hideout and wanted to surround it. Adrien and I took the left-hand flank. Very soon we ran slap into an African poacher. Adrien pointed his pistol at him and cried 'Stop!' The African let out a scream, turned tail and fled. In hot pursuit we very

---

[1] A tiny animal believed by zoologists, oddly enough, to be a relative of the elephant.

Next to eating, sleeping is the gorillas'
main activity. Adrien de Schryver's work has
banished forever the gorillas' King Kong image.

Adrien and 'Broken Arm'.

nearly met our deaths. As he ran from us the poacher had had time to plant his spear at an angle of forty-five degrees into the path. Adrien swerved and avoided it by a hair's breadth. It only ripped his shirt; another inch and it would have pierced his heart.

After a while, having re-grouped, we found the poachers' hut, abandoned. It was stacked with food and skins. We burned it to the ground as a warning. Later the poachers were caught and fined. Adrien's attitude was somewhat ambivalent: after all, he said, it was only a short time since the park had been the poachers' lawful hunting ground. They must be taught a lesson, but not too harshly. But then Adrien was an exceptionally magnanimous man.

One day we saw two young gorillas playing on a tree. Adrien helped me to set up my tripod. The resulting photograph would be infinitely better than one taken with a hand-held camera, and a shaking hand at that. I was so intent on what I was doing that I did not notice I was standing on a safari ants' nest. In a very short time hundreds of these tiny creatures came crawling up my legs, right to the upper, more private regions. I grew increasingly uncomfortable, but the gorillas were playing so enchantingly that I tried to lessen the irritation by gyrating my body like a beat singer, while still looking through the camera. Adrien confessed later that he could not help laughing.

Just as the gorillas embarked on a play-fight all the little intruders seemed to bite at the same time. The scene I had through the viewfinder was remarkable, but so too was the pain. How long could I stand it? Finally the gorillas made up my mind for me and left the tree. With lightning speed I pulled down my pants and moved away from the nest. Then I started to pick the ants off one by one. Some of them had locked their jaws so tightly that the body came away without the head. Even then the severed head went on biting for a few minutes.

There was a repeat performance with a different cast later, when Lee's attractive girlfriend, Carol Cawthra, a photographic model, came to see the gorillas. We walked a long way without seeing the animals. Then suddenly Adrien motioned us to freeze. He had seen the ants' nest, and Lee and Carol were standing right in it. He told them to be quite quiet and not to move. They followed his instructions exactly. Soon their bodies started to gyrate. My camera was running. I never saw clothes come off so fast. The ants were everywhere and within seconds the girls stood there in only bras and panties, picking the ants off one by one. Fortunately they both had a good sense of humour and laughed the whole thing off.

One day we watched the Kasimir family cross a road that ran through the park. As we stood at the foot of a steep embankment overgrown with wet vegetation we saw Kasimir climbing up towards the top, where the road wound through the forest. Adrien motioned to follow him and we clambered, slipping and sliding up the slope towards the road. We set up our camera equipment and waited. Parked on the other side of the road was Adrien's VW Combi. After ten minutes the bushes parted and Kasimir ran screaming on to the road, squatting down in the middle like a Buddha to ensure the safe passage of his family, who one by one crossed to the other side. He eyed the Combi speculatively and then charged it with a thunderous roar; but, seeing that it did not move, he climbed up the other side of the embankment and left the guard duty to Hannibal. Hannibal strode slowly across in a sideways manner which has been called the strutting walk. Broken Arm, a female, followed and the rearguard was brought up by Musharamina.

Kasimir crosses the road.

One day when some of Adrien's friends joined us we found the gorillas near a newly developed tree plantation. We followed them through dense jungle and overtook them among even denser vegetation. Then Adrien heard the three big males approaching; he motioned me to set up my tripod and we waited. One male was calling from the left, one from the right and Kasimir from the middle. The tension became unbearable. Adrien eyed the bushes, we eyed the bushes. The crackling of dead dried branches came nearer; short calls were exchanged between the three males. Then I could make out the huge bulk of Kasimir, who was following closely on our spoor. The communication between the males increased. Then all three males charged at once. I was filming, hand-holding the camera; but Adrien's friends panicked. They fell over each other and me and kept bumping my camera so that the final film was mostly unusable.

Kasimir threw some earth towards us. Musharamina was about two feet from Lee, displaying his enormous strength by snapping a small tree, and Hannibal ran past us screaming at the top of his voice, and drumming his giant hands on his chest. We were absolutely terrified. The gorillas had achieved their goal.

We stood there, our hearts racing. Only Adrien was quite calm, even if I did detect his face changing into a slightly worried expression during the confusion. Musharamina, obviously fascinated by the impression he was making, charged again. Then Adrien charged back. Musharamina instantly stopped. This was the only time I saw Adrien charge a gorilla. Musharamina turned away and the rest of the family followed. Perhaps they felt that Kasimir had made his point, and passage was now quite safe. They moved past in single file on both sides of us and vanished into the thicket beyond.

After this encounter Musharamina developed an annoying habit. As we moved through the bushes he used to wait in thick cover and watch us. When Adrien, Lee and I had passed he would suddenly leap out and charge the pygmies, who were thrown into utter confusion.

The pygmies thought we were crazy. Mushebere told us that he and his brother had eaten Kasimir's father, and that he was delicious. Adrien later confirmed this story, and added that a few years later Kasimir had found the two brothers together in the forest. He had managed to get hold of Mushebere's brother and had ripped him apart. It took Adrien several days to get to the corpse, as the gorillas refused to leave it.

Soon Hannibal staged for us a display almost as frightening as Kasimir's first charge. It was always Adrien who was charged – as if the gorillas had a love-hate relationship with him. Hannibal's charge was totally unexpected. We had been sitting quite close to a group of gorillas who were tolerating our presence and going about their business. Suddenly Hannibal hurled himself at Adrien's head. I thought it was the end. At the last possible moment Hannibal checked his blow. As he thundered past he tore at Adrien's shirt, then swerved back into the forest. The drama was enacted so swiftly that we didn't realize what had happened until we replayed it in slow-motion later.

In my six months with the gorillas I learned much about the habits of these huge and basically peaceful animals. When *Gorilla* (1974) was finally completed and shown on television, it proved one of the most successful in all the *Survival* series, and I believe Adrien really liked it.

Not long after I had left Bukavu Kasimir died, and a strange thing happened. Kasimir's wives and his whole family adopted Adrien as their leader, Kasimir's successor. Of course this bizarre situation could not last, but for a period of at least three weeks Adrien held the position of honorary head of the gorillas of Kahuzi-Biega.

It is sad that this story of the Lords of the Forest should have an unhappy ending, but so it turned out. Under a new law passed by President Mobutu it became illegal for private people to keep captive gorillas. Baby gorillas might have all the charm in the world, but even a half-grown animal would present many problems, including the expense of feeding it, and danger in handling it.

So when one day Adrien came across a tame baby gorilla that was being kept as a pet he felt obliged to confiscate it and bring it home. He knew that he had only two options. Either it must be given to a reliable zoo, or it must be returned to its native forests. Inevitably, given his character and beliefs, he chose the latter alternative. He took all the necessary precautions – the required injections to ensure that the baby was free, after its captivity, from all human diseases. What happened next is best described by quoting Lee's letter to Colin Willock.

'Adrien quietly said "What about taking Julie (mini gorilla) to visit Kasimir?" We could hardly believe we had heard right. We wanted more than anything to see what the reaction would be of the wild gorillas to a baby gorilla in our group, but everybody Adrien had talked to had advised him against it as the danger is too great both for himself and for the gorilla . . . I mean there is a good chance that the gorilla male would get angry (as he would if a strange gorilla family came into his territory) and would simply kill Adrien and Julie.'

'We were all pretty nervous Monday morning. Julie (the name is

Kasimir let out a terrifying scream, and then charged.

derived from "*Ngila*", the Swahili for gorilla) sat on Adrien's lap on the drive to the park. She was a little nervous, but no more than on other occasions away from home. We sat by the road while the pygmies went to find out exactly where the gorillas were, as we didn't want to tire her with extra walking. She then did a very strange thing. Usually in a new place she sits close to the people she knows, but that morning she walked alone into the middle of the road and sat down and cried as if she had been deserted. Then Adrien would go and pick her up or she would come back to sit on his lap. She seemed both more adventurous and more agitated than when we had ever seen her. We remarked on it, and Dieter got out the recorder to tape the sound. We had heard her yell when she was angry, but not like she was anguished.'

'The pygmies came back saying the gorillas were very near, but in a dense bad place, the place where Patrice's (the pygmy) brother had been killed by Kasimir. We had only walked ten minutes when we saw the bushes moving and Kasimir gave his usual "questioning bark". That really made Julie scared and she squirmed around in Adrien's arms and promptly had diarrhoea all over him. Patrice was clearing the bush for the tripod and Dieter was madly rushing to assemble the camera. We could see Hannibal watching us from the top of a bush and then he did something he had never done before. From fifteen yards he moved directly for us, stopping only when he was two yards away, his eyes glued on Julie. I had been trying to mop up the shit all over Adrien but gave up and froze next to Dieter, who was filming the approach of Hannibal, cursing that there wasn't time to set up the recorder.'

'Adrien picked up Julie from his feet where he had set her down for a moment and she wriggled in his arms and gave a little cry. That did it. Kasimir came straight for us and Hannibal moved aside to let him pass. Luckily we were in a bit of a clearing, because in the dense bush we would never have seen anything. When Kasimir saw Julie he started to scream, threw his weight on a bush and smashed it down, not charging but screaming, with Adrien screaming at him "Kasimir, Kasimir" and Julie really screaming too. It is the first time I have really been scared with the gorillas and Dieter says if the camera hadn't been on a tripod he would have been shaking too. This was no charge or show of force or demonstration, this was a real confrontation and Kasimir meant business.'

'Still screaming, Kasimir suddenly moved over the bush and rushed past us and sat-stood just in front of Adrien. Adrien saw that there was nothing he could do. Either Kasimir would take Julie away by force or he would have to put her down. If it was by force there was a good chance Kasimir would injure or kill him, and he had no idea what Kasimir would do with the little gorilla, but he had no real choice so he set Julie down at his feet. Kasimir was only a yard away and simply reached out his long arm and quite gently rolled Julie towards him. Still screaming he picked her up and tucked her under his arm and moved off on three "legs" to the spot, less than thirty feet away, where the rest of the family watched us. There he gently handed her to one of three females and she immediately started to caress and groom her. Kasimir just sat and watched them, then the family quietly moved away. From the first moment Hannibal had started for us to the end Dieter shot 100 feet of film, thus the whole scene took less than three minutes! Needless to say Dieter filmed the whole thing and that roll number 266 is worth its weight in gold.'

'We were really shaken, but felt it was important to talk about it, and Dieter had the sense to get the recorder so we could remember those first impressions. There was no way we could follow the family, that we were sure. We could hear Julie cry a little but soon she was quiet and the family probably all around her watching her. One big male was between us and the group, keeping an eye on us. After about half an hour we could hear them starting to feed and move off.'

'Our biggest question was immediately answered: "Would wild gorillas accept a young from another family?" Not only did they accept it, but they took it away. They saw immediately that there was a gorilla with us that did not belong to us and they took it. Our next question will still have to be answered: "Will Julie be able to survive with the change of diet, the cold, the rain, with none of the females lactating at the moment?'

'We all felt that in its own way it was the best solution for Julie. Even if she dies it is better there than in a zoo, which is the only alternative. The de Schryver family were all very upset to lose their sixth child; the kids really adored Julie, but I think they all agree that it is better for her.'

When Kasimir saw the baby gorilla he started screaming. Suddenly he rushed past us and crouched in front of Adrien. Adrien saw that there was nothing he could do, so he set Julie down at his feet. Kasimir simply reached out his long arm and quite gently rolled the baby towards him. Then, still screaming, he picked her up, tucked her under his arm and moved off to where the rest of the family stood watching.

Baby gorillas have all the charm in the world.

Right: Julie investigates my Arriflex 16 ST.

Alas Julie did not survive. The next day a storm of unusual violence for the time of year broke over the forest, with drenching rain and fierce winds. It lasted several days. When the storm abated the trackers returned to the neighbourhood where the kidnap had taken place. They saw a female feeding on leaves in the middle of the gorilla family group. Presently the group started to move on. The browsing female looked back and called. Nothing happened. She went back and reappeared with a limp bundle. It was Julie. She had survived for only ten days.

10 The Elephant and the Volcano

While I was staying with Adrien at Bukavu I had made up my mind to explore and photograph the great volcano of Mount Nyiragongo in the Virunga mountain range. In the closing days of my visit Professor Grzimek arrived, and we decided to make a reconnaissance flight over the volcano.

On the way we got a fine view of the huge lava flows which have been called 'the Elephant's Grave'. They were strewn with white bones and carcasses of elephants, hippopotami and many other African fauna. The flows were a form of gas chamber, for they had a very high concentration of carbon dioxide gas which penetrates the air above to a height of six feet. Low-flying birds literally fall unconscious from the sky.

With the Professor I also visited Rwindi, the headquarters of the Virunga National Park. The Professor had always been a great supporter of this park. One of his main contributions was the Lumbimbi Scientific Institute, which he had set up with money from the Frankfurt Zoological Society. In Zaire his name was almost a household word, for it was at the park's camp of Ishango at the mouth of the Semliki river that he had made his famous film *No Place for Wild Animals*.

From Ishango we went on to Vitshumbi, situated at the lakeshore inside the Virunga National Park. This was no ordinary village. Its lake teemed with hippopotami and fish. The people of Vitshumbi lived by fishing, and were on terms of complete familiarity with the animals around them.

One day I saw an elephant sauntering up a street there. A pole was protruding from one of the thatched huts. When the elephant reached it

The elephants of Vitshumbi were used to rubbing shoulders with the villagers, who paid them scant attention.

he stopped and began to scratch his back on it. As he moved his body to and fro so the hut swayed to his rhythm. No one seemed surprised, or even much to mind. I also saw a male hippo charging up the main street in pursuit of a female of the species. The crowds scattered – but not in fear, just to get out of the way. The hippo had no evil intentions and ignored the bustling activity around it.

The Belgian manager of the fishing concession for Vitshumbi had a fine house with a close-cropped lawn stretching down to the lake. When I admired the condition of the turf I was told that every day a hippo appeared on the lawn, grazed contentedly for an hour or so, and then departed.

Each catch of fish, as it was unloaded, was laid out on what passed for a quay. Here the buying and selling took place, with all the accompanying African barter. But behind the human hagglers stood a row of pelicans. They had come not to buy and sell and barter, but simply to steal. Every now and then when no one was looking one of them would waddle forward, seize a sizeable catch and fly off.

The elephants of Vitshumbi were used to rubbing shoulders with the villagers. It would be an exaggeration to say that they passed unnoticed in a crowd, but people paid them scant attention. As I found to my cost, it was another matter when someone *did* pay them attention. My particular elephant was standing alone in an open space about half a mile from the village. He was a magnificent specimen and Professor Grzimek wanted me to photograph him. I took my stance about seventy-five yards away, motioning Lee and Professor Grzimek to a safe distance. I was wearing a battery belt around my waist, plugged by cable to the camera and tripod. I did not realize that I was virtually the tripod's prisoner. Without warning the elephant charged. I wanted desperately to run, but I was trapped in my battery belt. I could not loosen it in time.

In desperation I threw up my hands and yelled at the charging beast. He was within three feet of me. For an instant the elephant halted in his tracks, turned his attention to smashing the tripod and trampling the camera into the ground. In that instant I managed to pull the cable out of the belt and ran for dear life. The elephant pursued me for about a hundred yards and then desisted. But for that instant's pause I would certainly have died. It was Professor Grzimek who took the photograph – a real action picture. After a safe interval I went to see whether irretrievable damage had been done to the camera. The lens was badly

Without warning the elephant charged:
but I was trapped.

*The lake of lava suddenly
rose about a hundred feet
and giant bubbles burst,
an inferno of fire
and light.*

bent, and the camera was full of dirt, but it still worked – a tribute to the makers of Arriflex.

Afterwards I told Lee that this must be a lesson to both of us: we must never again let ourselves be trapped like this when using a tripod. But it was a lesson that Lee tragically did not learn.

Lee had been my assistant now for two and a half years, and we were very close. Nevertheless the time had come when she decided she wanted to work on her own. She agreed that I always made sure she got the maximum credit for the work she did with me, but that was not good enough – she wanted to make films that were all hers.

So when Anglia Television asked me if I thought she was ready to start on her own I said yes. We decided that her first assignment should be a film about the hippos that abounded in the Virunga Park, some of which we had encountered in Vitshumbi. So we went to one of the big hippo wallows about six miles from Vitshumbi and there set up a hide on the banks of the pond, into which Lee and her camera and tripod vanished. As I drove away in my jeep a herd of hippos started to surround the hide. 'She really is a brave girl,' I thought.

My objective was a pride of lions which I had glimpsed on our way, on a buffalo kill. If I could chase the lions off the kill and pull the carcass up to the hippo wallow Lee might get some splendid film footage. It was easy to locate the kill: vultures showed me the way. It was far from easy to get hold of the carcass. Seven lions and three cubs were eating. At my approach they retreated, snarling.

I drove slowly and deliberately until the buffalo's horns were almost touching the car. The lions were now about fifty feet away. Slowly I opened the door and leaned out to fix a rope round the horns. The lioness of the party charged to within six feet of me, her tail flapping from side to side. From past experience I was pretty certain that this was only a mock-charge, so I looked her straight between the eyes; a quick retreat could have been fatal. Carefully I tied the rope round the buffalo's horns and then, watching the lioness with equal care, moved back into the jeep and closed the door. I now moved off, dragging the carcass behind me, the lioness following at a distance.

Fifteen minutes later we reached the hippo wallow and Lee's hide. I dropped the carcass behind the encircling hippos and waited. After a very short time the lions appeared, cautiously at first, then as hunger took control the pride started eating, watched by a pool full of wallowing hippos. One of the cubs, seized with the curiosity natural to all young things, started to stalk towards them. One of the hippos then rose to its feet. That was enough for the cub, who retreated rapidly to the shelter of its pride.

Lee and I carried on filming for several days. Then I felt it was time to fulfil my promise and leave her on her own. I bade her farewell and wished her good luck, before proceeding to the Nyiragongo volcano.

My companion in this venture, Jacques Durieux, was a Belgian who had formerly been a teacher and was now a tour guide based in Goma. He had been studying volcanoes for several years and had taken in many expeditions. With his help and expertise I planned to make a film of Nyirangongo's active crater.

After several hours of driving from Rwanda we reached our objective, the five-thousand-foot Mount Nyiragongo. The last rays of the sun were striking its peak as we arrived. A column of smoke rose vertically into the sky. Night fell, and soon the crimson glow of the lava was reflected like a huge searchlight.

When morning dawned, the mountain was shrouded in mist and cloud. With the twenty-three porters Jacques had hired we started up the narrow trail that led to the summit. It took us five hours to reach the rim of the crater, and by then the sun was shining. The view was stupendous. The main crater is about five hundred feet deep and a mile across. It is formed of a solid sheet of lava and is inactive; but another five hundred feet below it is a smaller crater, about two hundred yards in diameter. It was with this crater that we were concerned. It was, to say the least of it, highly active. It had become the real volcano.

Our first problem was with the porters. They flatly refused to climb down the steep ridge that led to the main crater. The mountain was the home of their gods, and if they desecrated it in this way they would never return. So Jacques and I had to spend the whole afternoon carrying our equipment and supplies down to the bottom of the crater, listening all the time to the menacing, thunderous noise of bubbling lava below. Exhausted, we camped in the late evening, next to the foot of the wall. As night fell the turmoil and thundering sounded to me like the forces of hell. I felt like a tiny insignificant speck, an unimportant spectator of the scene before us.

Jacques was used to all this, but to me it was as if I were witnessing the creation of earth, its very beginning. For a while the thundering stopped and there were only a few explosions. Then suddenly the lava lake rose about a hundred feet and giant bubbles burst, raining ash upon us. Fresh explosions followed, making the lake an inferno of fire and light.

The next day we planned to go inside the active crater. Jacques and I

Overleaf: As we climbed into Nyiragongo's active crater the lava bubbled menacingly below.

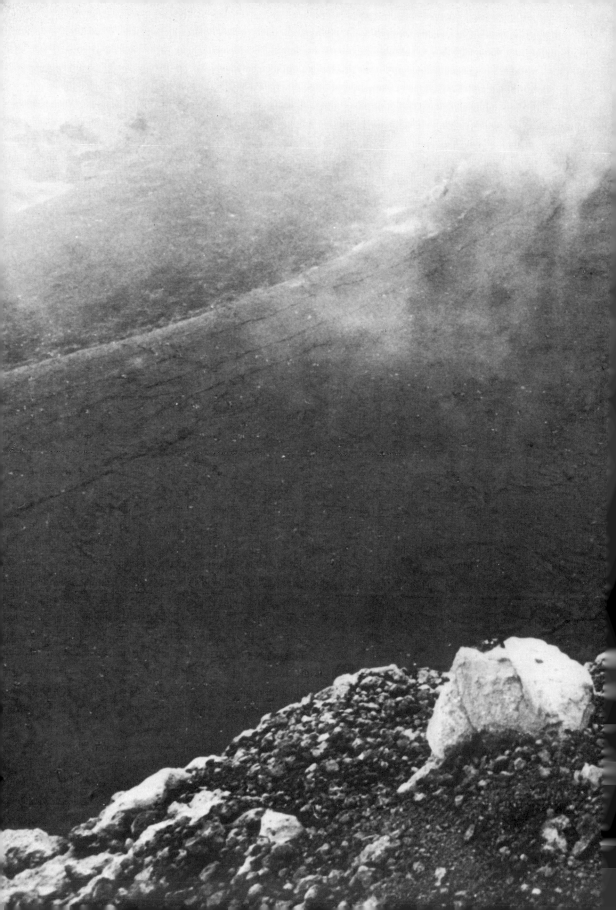

both wore asbestos suits and gas masks which enabled us to survive in a place where there was no other life. We got to within fifty yards of the inner crater, but no further: the heat was unbearable. I had to hold my camera behind my back in order to keep it as cool as possible. If I wanted to film I had to move it quickly in front of me, take the shot and move it back.

Then we started moving down into the crater. Breathing through our gas masks, we got to the edge. As quickly as we could we hurried over some sulphur-covered rocks which were emitting poisonous fumes, until we reached a further jagged outcrop. Slowly we climbed down, below us the thundering explosions of the lava. One slip would be fatal. Silently I prayed that, if I fell, I might at least be unconscious before plunging into the liquid lava.

We reached a flat area with very few rocks, which sounded hollow. The lava was flowing beneath it. Jacques went in front and I followed. We approached a hole in the ground, about five feet in diameter, which was emitting a forceful jet of gas and steam. Jacques moved in and held his sampler into the escaping gases, while I filmed him.

Then the vertical cliff in front of him started to collapse. The rocks crashed on to the thin floor we were standing on. Jacques got up, saw a crack widening and escaped just in time. The ground he had been standing on collapsed and crashed into the lava below. He ran towards me on a platform of solidified lava, jumping over cracks in which lava flowed. When we reached solid rock Jacques measured the temperature of the fiery gases blasting out from a nearby hole; they were 4416° Fahrenheit in the centre. I was sweating profusely under my gas mask, which made it difficult to look through the viewfinder.

Suddenly the ground parted beneath us. We jumped to one side. It was the right one; on the other we would have been isolated in a lake of lava, and there would have been no escape. The crack grew wider and wider and the lava rose in it. Deadly gases streamed from all sides. I held on to my camera and filmed. The acid fumes had misted even the chrome on my Arriflex. It became more difficult to breathe, as it takes some effort to pull air in through the gas mask filter.

We decided to move back. When Jacques was already halfway up the embankment of loose rocks, I slipped and fell. My head hit the ground, which didn't matter as I was wearing a helmet; but the blow knocked off my gas mask and just a whiff of toxic gases entered my lungs. I thought they were going to burst.

The stinging pain in my lungs became almost unbearable. I saw colours and weird shapes. And then I had visions. *Survival* Anglia's New York President, Jack Ball, appeared before me, saying that if I came out

Nothing quite like it.

of this alive he would introduce me to the most beautiful girl in New York. Then he vanished among the ashes. What an incentive!

Desperately I groped for the gas mask, managed to get it back on and breathed in with a gasp of relief. Then I regained full consciousness and saw that Jacques was on his way down to help me out of the inferno.

When I saw Jack Ball and told him this story later, he was very amused.

11 Escape from Zaire

14 May 1974 was my thirty-eighth birthday. I had been filming at Mount
Nyiragongo for twenty-one days. On that day the lava had risen and for
some strange reason the noise had subsided. Just as I was about to focus
my camera I heard a voice calling from the rim of the top crater. It was
one of the guards, waving a letter in his hand. I finished my scene, put the
tripod and the camera over my shoulder and Jacques Durieux and I
slowly made our way back to the small crater's rim, dodging the poisonous gases streaming from cracks in solidified lava. Leaving the cameras
in our little tents we scaled the six hundred feet of straight wall and
arrived on top of the crater to receive the letter the guard was holding. It
was from the Director of Technique Conservation Department of Zaire,
Mr Mburanumwe, asking me to report to him immediately in Goma.

Having been in Africa for years, and knowing how easily bureaucratic
problems can arise, I immediately expected the worst. I told Jacques that
I would set out at once, and would see him the following day at twelve
o'clock at the guard camp at the foot of the mountain. I was afraid our
film was going to be confiscated, and went through my shotlist book to
look at reels I could spare if need be. I quickly filmed a few more reels at
random, and packed these into a separate box. I could give these to the
officials. I packed the major reels into our rucksacks in between the
sleeping bags.

Then I left the site and proceeded on my way. A howling wind blew
tiny particles of volcanic dust into my eyes and in the distance I saw
Goma situated at the north end of the beautiful Lake Kivu, covered by a
slight haze. I couldn't help wondering what was about to happen to me.

I negotiated the first five hundred feet down the ash-covered side of
the crater and arrived at the halfway hut which was provided for tourists.
I re-tied my shoe-laces and started walking down the narrow path to the
bottom. I finally reached the guard post at the bottom of the mountain,
exhausted and with blisters forming on my feet. I got into Jacques' VW

Combi and turned the key, but nothing happened. The gears seemed to be jammed. No matter what I did I could not get it to start.

I had no alternative but to set out on foot, leaving the film and equipment behind. As it turned out it was lucky that I did. With my feet aching I began to walk. Amazed African faces met me on my way: a white man on foot? It was incredible. Walking through villages I was stared at like a creature from another planet. My feet really started to ache and I took a rest. The thirst began to bite in my mouth. Wasn't there a clear stream around somewhere? I undid my laces and took off my boots. In some places the blisters had opened and started to bleed.

Unfortunately there was a petrol shortage in Zaire, and that was why there were no trucks on the road. Suddenly I heard the droning of a vehicle in the distance. A jeep approached, and it stopped right next to me. It was loaded with goats, and police officers armed with automatic FN rifles. I feared there might have been a coup. I put on the friendliest expression I could, and asked the driver for a lift. He told me to jump on the back. The policemen were friendly, and slowly my fear that they were looking for me diminished. I sat between two goats and two officers, who waved the muzzles of their FN guns right in front of my face. We bounced along the road, and after thirty minutes reached the outskirts of Goma. I jumped down, not forgetting to leave *matabiche* behind me.

I set off towards the office of Mr Mburanumwe. A commando of MPLA Jeunesse, President Mobutu's Youth Movement, came marching along the street singing '*Mobutu Sese Seko Kuku Ngbendu Was Sa Banga*' and carrying a picture of Mobutu. As I crossed the road in front of them, an irate, fanatical voice stopped me in my tracks. I turned round and walked quietly back to where the voice had come from. The speaker must have been about twenty-two years old, and had Mobutu pictures all over his green shirt. He wore sunglasses and an American baseball cap, and had a whistle in his mouth. When I got closer the Jeunesse group surrounded me.

The man screamed that I had turned my back to the President, in whose honour they were marching. I apologized, saying this was certainly not my intention, and that I would make up for it. I pushed my way through the line, walked back to the side of the road I had come from, and as the group watched me I walked across again backwards, *facing* the picture of President Mobutu. Everyone was happy; they quickly fell back into line and went on singing down the road.

A few minutes later I arrived at Mr Mburanumwe's office. He appeared quite friendly at first, but then he reached into his desk and pulled out a typewritten piece of paper which said that Professor

Grzimek's team must suspend all its operations immediately, and that all film would be confiscated. So my fears in this respect had been well founded. I acted as if I could not understand, simply to win time. I told him that I must go and collect my equipment from Nyiragongo.

Needless to say I spent a sleepless night. The next day I went to collect my Unimog from the garage where it had been serviced. As I drew out of Goma towards the Nyirangongo guard camp I noticed a green VW Combi following me at a discreet distance. I realized that if I was to get any film out of the country I had to come up with a very quick idea. I could not try to shake off my pursuers, as this would imply that I had something to hide.

Suddenly I had the solution. I watched the road for a very dense patch of forest which was to be the key to my plan. This I found immediately after a tight bend. I noted a few landmarks on which I could orientate myself in order to find it again on my way back.

I arrived at the camp, where Jacques had just arrived with the equipment we had left at the mountain, including the latest films I had taken. I put the expendable reels in a cardboard box on the back seat of the Unimog, and I put the 'real' ones in a rucksack, adding an empty carton. We loaded all the equipment into the truck under the watchful eye of the guards.

I drove off, still followed by the green VW. Suddenly, as we approached a bend, I grabbed the empty carton and flung it out of the window into the bush. I drove on, watching the reactions of my pursuers in the mirror. Everything went according to plan: they stopped in order to retrieve the carton. Meanwhile I accelerated round the bend, towards the dense patch of forest. Here I flung out the rucksack containing the films and drove on. I slowed down, and soon the green car appeared again.

At Goma I walked in to the office and delivered the expendable film, hoping that Mr Mburanumwe would think he had got what he wanted. Instead he got very angry and said that he wanted *all* the film. I told him that I did not have any more. He got angrier still; he made me sit down and told me that there were ways and means in Zaire to make a man talk.

I looked around at the rather large armed guards, and realized that I was getting into deep trouble. Mburanumwe was working himself up into a rage. He told his guards to unload all my equipment and confiscate it. When the guards started throwing my equipment on the ground I got really upset. I told him that I hoped he understood that he was about to start an international diplomatic incident. This seemed to have an effect. I told him that Professor Grzimek was a member of the West German Government, and that his actions might have serious repercussions.

For a moment Mburanumwe hesitated, as if to think what he should do. Then he told the guards to load the equipment back into the truck. His tone changed and he became more friendly. I told him that I must now go to Virunga to fetch Lee, in order to comply with the official instructions, and that I would return in a few days.

He agreed, and allowed me to go to my car. Jacques and I set out for Virunga. As we were passing the airport I saw a familiar face, an Englishman whom I had met at Kahuzi-Biega with Adrien de Schryver. I stopped and asked him if he would take my films back to England for me. He agreed. Jacques and I quickly drove to the place where the sack of films was hidden. After making sure we were not being followed, we picked it up, brought it back to Goma and gave it to my anonymous friend.

Relieved that my films were now safe, Jacques and I went on along the appalling road from Goma to the Virunga National Park. Jacques and I decided that we should go and get Lee and all the equipment, but not return to Mburanumwe.

Late in the afternoon we reached Virunga. Lee had already packed all her equipment and we loaded it into my Unimog and her VW Combi. The next morning we set out again. Jacques went with Lee, and I was on my own. We arranged to meet at five o'clock on the Bukavu road, twenty miles from Goma, if we got through.

As I entered Goma I saw the green Combi again, and immediately knew I was being followed. Damn it, I thought, what to do? I circled some of the roundabouts, drove back into town, but still had my pursuers on my heels.

Suddenly the opportunity came: a large truck pulled out of a side street and began to reverse in order to make a turn. I heard the Combi hooting frantically and I accelerated round a corner. When I looked into the rear view mirror the Combi had disappeared. I made straight for the road to Bukavu.

A little way out of town on the right was the Mercedes garage. I turned quickly into it and parked the truck out of sight I leapt out and hid behind a door where I could watch the road. Soon the Combi appeared, followed by a jeep – was it the police? They went past, heading for Bukavu. I breathed a sigh of relief.

In order to kill time I asked the mechanic to weld my petrol can bracket into place. Meanwhile I watched from the workshop hoping to see the two cars return. After about an hour they did. They must have given up the chase: they were going back to Goma. When the welding was done I filled up with diesel fuel and headed towards Bukavu, still anxiously watching my mirror for the dreaded green Combi.

After twenty miles I stopped to wait for Lee. At about five o'clock her Combi appeared on the road. As she stopped we heard an aeroplane flying low towards us. The army? No, it was Adrien who by now had heard about our situation and who wanted to see if we needed help. We waved, indicating that we were OK, and he flew on. After munching a few bananas we drove on towards Bukavu.

Night came quickly, as it does in Africa, and soon our headlights had to be switched on. Lee had warned me that the road was very bad. When midnight came we stopped beside the road; Lee got out the stove and made some tea. It tasted wonderful, and gave us new energy for the trip that was to come. The distance to Bukavu was only 120 miles, but it seemed endless. We half expected to come upon a police road block. On and on we ground along the twisting, turning road.

It was two o'clock in the morning when we came upon a lorry stuck in the middle of the road. There had been a landslide: the road was covered with muddy, greasy black soil. I stopped the Unimog and Lee and I walked through knee-deep mud to investigate. It looked hopeless. About a mile of road was covered: twelve trucks were stuck. Each one had its back wheels hanging over the edge of the road.

I spoke to one of the drivers: I knew I could not help him get back on to the road, but maybe I could winch some of the trucks out of the way, in order to clear a path through. The drivers all agreed that I should try. I unwound the winch from my Unimog, hooked it on to one of the trucks and started to back up. I managed to pull it a little to one side but my Unimog nearly slid into the side ditch in the process.

I stopped and got out, realizing it was hopeless. The only way to pull some of these vehicles free was from the front. But I was behind. I walked along between the trucks and realized that my only chance of driving to the front of the line was to put differential lock on all four wheels with cross-country reduction gear. It would be like skiing in a zig-zag through six slalom gates. I reckoned I had a fifty-fifty chance.

I walked back and got into the Unimog, which was named Samson. I patted him on the engine cowling and said, 'Samson, this is it. If we get stuck, we may never get out of here.'

I started the engine, put him into gear, gave him another pat, and off we went.

The engine was going at full revs to have maximum power. The vehicle swerved on the greasy surface. Then I flung the wheel to the left. In order to pass the truck I had to go down into the ditch on the left side of the road. As I slid into it I turned the wheel back to the right, but Samson could not make it, he was still going straight. The next truck was coming closer, its back wheels totally submerged in the black quagmire. I was only about twenty feet from the truck when Samson's tyres found a grip and he lurched to the right, making his way up the middle of the road. As fast as I could I turned the steering wheel back to straighten out the wheels in the mud. I was crossing the road at an angle of about forty-five degrees.

Reaching the middle of the road I immediately slid towards the right-hand ditch. Samson's wheels were now flinging mud all over. The next truck loomed up. At first there was no reaction from the wheels, which I was trying to turn left. There was no grip; we were just sliding. I nearly hit the truck, but again at the last moment the wheels gripped.

I slalomed through nine more trucks standing criss-cross along the road. I stopped. Immediately there was a clamour of African voices asking me to help them get back on the road. We tried, but after several unsuccessful attempts all we could do was move the trucks out of the middle of the road in order to pull the Combi through.

At last, at four o'clock in the morning, we arrived at Bukavu. We went straight to Adrien's house. A few hours later I went to see the German Consul to tell him the story and to store some of the equipment.

I wanted to leave Bukavu as soon as possible, but Lee decided to stay. After we parted I arranged to get a lift to Rwanda. We arrived at the border post after lunch and I ran into the office to get all the formalities completed as quickly as possible. Suddenly the telephone rang and my heart started thumping. The officer spoke to someone. He put the phone down. Now it was my turn. As he opened my passport the phone rang again. I started to get really worried. He looked at me and put the phone down, mumbling. Just as he stamped the passport and signed it a soldier came running into the room with his FN automatic. I thought, this is it! But he walked straight past me and deposited the rifle in the corner; it had started raining heavily and he didn't want the rifle to get wet.

I went outside into the rain and got back into the car. I wasn't out of the country yet. As we moved towards the barrier a soldier stopped us. He looked at our pass for a while, as rain dripped on it. Then he gave the signal. The barrier opened. I was in Rwanda.

Epilogue

Soon after my 'escape from Zaire' it was explained to me that the whole incident had been a bureaucratic blunder. The film that I had made in the country, of Adrien de Schryver and the gorillas, was shown in London to the Zaire Ambassador, and when he was given a copy for President Mobutu, he expressed much pleasure. Soon after this the president ordered a 2500-square mile extension of the Kahuzi-Biega National Park; and I like to think that our film encouraged him to continue the conservation work that was being done in his country.

It was not long after this that I left Africa for the last time. I had worked there for eighteen years: I had filmed some of its most beautiful and astonishing sights; and I had made friends with some of its greatest conservationists.

But now Asia beckoned. For if the films I had made for *Survival* had helped to emphasize the plight of African wildlife, how much greater was the need where Asia was concerned – where animals like the Bengal tiger, the one-horned rhinoceros and the orang-utan were already seriously threatened. So, with the consent and indeed encouragement of *Survival*, I was Asia-bound.

One of my last adventures in Africa was learning to fly a plane; and as soon as I had my licence I bought a Cessna 206 in which I planned to make the several-thousand mile journey from Kenya to Kathmandu.

Early one morning my friend Bill Holz and I took off from Nairobi's Wilson airport, heading north towards Addis Ababa. Flying past the flank of Mount Kenya I bade farewell to the fantastically beautiful country that bears its name. Four hours later we were over Lake Shala. I was anxious to see what had happened to the pelicans since I had filmed them five years ago. They were there still, in all the whiteness of their soaring flight. I could see too the island in the lake where they nested. I was relieved to see that the colony seemed to have grown larger and there was no sign of human activity in the neighbourhood. In the troubled days through which Ethiopia was living it seemed a good sign.

We refuelled in Addis Ababa and took off for Djibouti, arriving in the dark. It was the last place in Africa where we would sleep. Tomorrow a chapter embracing all my adult life would come to its close. We took off at dawn, climbing north, heading towards Danakil country. In the distance I could see the great shimmering surface of Lake Abbe, where I had finished my Danakil film. Now, I knew, below me all was changed. The Sultan of the Danakil was engaged in a bitter and bloody revolt against the new rulers in Addis Ababa, who had deposed and then murdered the Emperor. The Danakil, to my certain knowledge, were a wild and merciless tribe. But were they any worse than the Dergue, the new rulers who claimed to be the new *masters* of Ethiopia?

We flew on, over the Red Sea, heading towards Jiddah in Saudi Arabia. In the haze to our left Africa vanished, and on the right a new land emerged, the continent of Asia. Many flying hours later we touched down on the airfield of Kathmandu – where, looking out towards the great circle of the Himalayas, embracing Everest in the east and Annapurna in the west, I have written this book.

My African story cannot have a happy ending. It ends with personal tragedy, and another of greater dimensions. After I left I was never to see Lee Lyon again. One day she was waiting to film a young elephant which was being translocated to the Kagera National Park in Rwanda. She was attached to her tripod by a battery belt. As the door of its crate was opened the elephant charged. Unlike me, Lee was not able to free herself from the belt in time. She was trampled to death. It was a bitter loss for everyone who knew and worked with her.

During and since my eighteen years in Africa I have witnessed its birthpains of independence – its coups, civil wars and strife. Every paper in the world has carried headlines about its struggle for freedom and the political aspirations of its people. We condemn this leader because he bought a golden bed in Europe, this one because he has amassed a huge fortune in Switzerland, the next because he has ordered the slaughter of tens of thousands of his subjects. Since I left, more than 120 coups and attempted coups have taken place in Africa, forty of them resulting in military dictatorships or one-party rulers. There have been dozens of civil wars, millions of refugees, and mounting problems of food production and outright starvation.

While its countries are locked in ideological arguments, and fruitless political discussions – which party should rule, or which ruler should ally with whom – while 'super powers' wrestle to gain influence and meddle in its affairs, supplying weapons of war, causing destruction and misery of immeasurable proportions, the giant is bleeding to death. It is being drained not only of human blood, but of its water, its forests and its grazing land. The deserts are advancing in Africa at a frightening speed. And not only in Africa. An observer at a recent western environmental conference commented: 'So much political sniping and hollow hyperbole goes on that you begin to feel one of the greatest deserts is the human mind'.

The tide of sand is nullifying the efforts of African nations to produce larger crops for a better future, relentlessly destroying the basis of their existence. In 1970 nature hit back with disastrous results: drought and famine took the lives of more than 100,000 people living on the fringes of the southern Sahara. Modern methods of ploughing cut so deeply into the soil that it dried like dust; the winds caught it and just carried it away.

Deforestation has caused desertification, and livestock have destroyed the last bits of vegetation. While billions are spent on useless arms, largely for prestige purposes, little is done to halt the destruction of land and forests and conserve water supplies – the very basis of life.

As cattle mean wealth to the African peasant, whose numbers are anyway increasing, so the cattle, goats, sheep, and camels increase, needing more and more grazing and water. In the last fifty years 250,000 square miles of valuable land has been swallowed up by the Sahara. Years ago in the Sahel quarter United Nations experts drilled wells for the local nomads to water their livestock. The result was that the local population, which was increasing at an alarming rate anyway, acquired even more cattle, goats and camels. The animals converged from miles around, trampling all the vegetation and eating the very last roots of the soil, and the water table sank until there was only brackish water left.

Now again in the Sahel there are plans afoot to plant trees – but what about the millions of goats there? Is every seedling going to be fenced in?

All over the world mountains and hillsides are being denuded of forest as more land is brought under cultivation. The forest used to bind the soil together, shield it from the heat of the sun, and act as a sponge which slowly released water bit by bit throughout the year. With the forest gone the springs coming out of the hillsides stop, catching the land in the vicious circle of flood and drought. The rains rush down the slopes, taking the precious topsoil with them. It is not long before the resulting erosion changes a once fertile hillside into a desert, leaving only the rocks resembling a carcass devoured by scavengers and the bones left in the sun to bleach.

Whenever man has meddled with the balance of nature the results have been disastrous. When will we learn? If we abuse nature we will have to pay, one day. Pollution of the air, the sea, overpopulation, destruction of our habitat – these are all cheques drawn on the future. For centuries we have lived on the capital nature provided us with. Decades ago we used it up; now all the cheques increase the overdraft. One day we shall have to pay whether we like it or not.

You may ask what all this has got to do with wildlife; and if there are all these pressing problems why worry about wilderness areas and national parks?

Wildlife reserves and wilderness areas are our only visible remaining link with true nature. Managed and protected, they are among the few inexhaustible resources a country can have. In the future, as more and more of these areas fall to the axe and the plough, this will be even more true. True wild places provide us with a connection to our heritage. If we destroy that connection we shall drift about aimlessly, like orphans looking for the parents they never knew.

DIETER PLAGE'S FILMS
Made for Anglia Television's *Survival*

1968   *First Catch Your Unicorn*
1970   *Skeleton Coast*
1970   *The Long Dry Summer*
1970   *Striped Horse with a Red Collar*
1970   *The VIP's*
1970   *Death of a Zebra*
1970   *Okavango*
1971   *The Fence*
1971★ *Now or Never*
1971★ *Pelican Flyway*
1972★ *Air Support*
1972   *Miracle at Tendaho (Mitchell Cotts Film)*
1972   *Citizens of the Coral*
1973   *Airlift*
1973★ *The Forbidden Desert of the Danakil*
1973★ *The Family that Lived with Elephants*
1974★ *Gorilla* – Special Jury Award for the best network documentary, USA
       San Francisco Film Festival 1975
       Diploma at Ekofilm Czechoslovakic
1974   *Cat out of the Bag*
1975   *The Cry of the Fish Eagle*
1975★ *Balloon Safari* (with Alan Root)
1975   *Twelve Hours at the Waterhole*
1976   *The Great One Horned Rhinoceros*
1976★ *Orang Utan Orphans of the Forest* –
       1977 Christopher Award, USA
       1977 Ohio State Award, USA
       Diploma at Ekofilm Czechoslovakie
1977   *Elephant's Eye View*
1977★ *Tiger Tiger*
1978   *Distant Relations*
1978   *Tough Near the Top*
1978★ *The Leopard that Changed its Spots*
1978   *Follow that Tiger*
1979★ *The Last Round Up*

★   One-hour programmes

EQUIPMENT

Like many other young film makers I started off with a clockwork Bolex H16. I still have it, and use it as a standby when the batteries of my other cameras run down. Using its hand crank, I can simply carry on filming. But however well it is made the Bolex could not stand up to the constant pounding and hundreds of thousands of feet of film I use. So as soon as I could afford it I bought an Arriflex 16M camera. This has been my mainstay throughout the years I have filmed for *Survival*. It has never let me down: it has never jammed.

Later I added an Arriflex 16ST with the TTL light-meter. This camera, especially when used with hundred-foot rolls, is extraordinarily strong. When mine got trampled into the ground by an elephant the lenses were broken but all the camera needed was a good clean. It has worked ever since.

With the Arri turret I use the Angenieux F2.2 12–120 zoom, F5 200mm tele lens, and the Astro F5 300mm tele lens. I have found this the most useful combination, and it is perfectly adequate for good light conditions – especially in Africa. While I was making *Gorilla* in the jungles of Zaire, the available light was so low that I added an Astro F2 250mm lens and an Astro F2 150mm lens. Even then, I had to force-process some of the film under-exposed one to two stops.

At about that time Arriflex launched the dream of all cameramen, the beautiful Arriflex 16SR. This is an almost silent camera – so important when filming shy animals. Together with my SR I bought a 10–100mm Zeiss Vario Sonnar, and a 12–240 Angenieux Zoom with the beautiful Arri Power Zoom. Hand zooming may be all right for fast moving action, but for peaceful scenes a power zoom is essential.
tial.

For high speed filming I use an Eclair GV16, which takes speeds of up to 200 frames per second – sufficient for most wildlife filming. It is awkwardly constructed, but it has one very important advantage over other high speed cameras: it starts to full speed within a quarter of a second. Most other high speed cameras need two to four seconds 'run up time'.

For sound recordings I started with a Uher: but again, the terrible punishment my equipment has to take made this unusable very soon. I invested, wisely, in a Nagra IVL, the 'Rolls Royce' of all tape-recorders. Their quality and reliability is legendary. I was not so lucky with the Nagra SN, and even after lengthy and expensive repairs I am still trying to get a really good recording with it.

I am a firm believer in tripods, and use the Miller Professional and Senior heads with Cine 60 snap plates, which makes for quick changing of cameras. As for legs, I prefer the wooden Arri legs, as they are the most stable.

My longer telephoto lenses are a F5.6 500mm Zeiss Tessar (which is really designed for the Rolleiflex SL66, but I had it adapted for the Arriflex) and an Astro F6.3 1000mm lens which, although cumbersome, is useful for certain otherwise unobtainable shots.

Battery belts for wildlife filming are not so useful; the first one I owned nearly cost me my life. I now strap them around my waist only to carry them from A to B. Otherwise I always hang them on the tripod.

For still photography I use two Nikon FTN's and an F2 – all with motordrive. I have a good range of lenses, but find that I use the Nikon F2.8 180mm most. Lately I have added a Nikon FE with motordrive to my equipment. For very shy animals, I use the incomparably silent Leica M3.

In the 2¼ square department I first used the Rolleiflex SL66, which gave me excellent results, but I soon missed the motordrive. Recently I changed to a Hasselblad 500 ELM with a F5.6 350mm Tessar and various other lenses. I had an adaptor made to use these lenses on the Arriflex to give me maximum flexibility.

INDEX

Note:
(B) = Botswana
(N) = Namibia
(Z) = Zaire

(E) = Ethiopia
(S) = S. Africa
(K) = Kenya
(T) = Tanzania